"'How nice of Blake to write this book just for me.' That's what you'll be saying after you read *Save the Cat! Strikes Back*. No matter if you're a newbie or a produced writer, Blake understands that the struggle never ends. Whether you're rewriting or getting rewritten, looking for representation or leaving your representation, he's got you covered. And on those days when you don't feel like writing and all you want to do is go on the Internet and 'research,' read his chapter on discipline, focus, and positive energy. I guarantee you will be up and writing. I love this book!"

> — Kriss Turner, Writer, *Something New*;
> Writer/Producer, *Sherri*, *Everybody Hates Chris*,
> *The Bernie Mac Show*

"Written in his signature witty, conversational style, Blake Snyder has given us another gem. As relevant to the novelist as it is to the screenwriter, this is a book no writer should be without. I've read all of Blake's books, and never begin a story without his insanely useful 'Beat Sheet' by my side, but this time, Snyder goes one step further, sharing his own personal transformation from struggling writer to one who's seen great success. From the most generous and genuine writer/teacher of our time, this book will inspire the reader to scale all of those seemingly insurmountable brick walls and keep going — to choose getting *better* over getting *bitter*. This book is a must read!"

> — Alyson Noël, #1 *New York Times*
> Bestselling Author, *Evermore*, *Blue Moon*,
> *Shadowland*

"A dazzling expansion on Blake's original insights, this essential screenwriting tool is practical and profound."

> — Mark Hentemann, Writer/Executive Producer,
> *Family Guy*

"*Save the Cat! Strikes Back* is Blake's best yet. It expands on his principles of storytelling in a breezy, colloquial style and gives us a deeper personal insight to the relentlessly positive mindset that powered his great success and his generous spirit. Blake's life was far, far too short, but his work and his inspiring legacy will remain timeless."

> — Rick Drew, *movieScope Magazine*

SAVE THE CAT!®
STRIKES
BACK

More Trouble for Screenwriter's to Get Into... and Out Of

BLAKE SNYDER

Published by Save the Cat!® Press

Cover Design:
Brian Blevins

Interior Book Design:
Gina Mansfield Design

Editor:
Brett Jay Markel

Photos on pages viii and 87, chart on page 47:
Peter Bennett/Ambient Images

Printed by McNaughton & Gunn, Inc.
Saline, Michigan

ISBN 10: 0-9841576-0-3
ISBN 13: 978-0-9841576-0-0

TABLE OF CONTENTS

ix   FOREWORD

xiii   THE INTRODUCTION:
OH, YOU'RE IN TROUBLE NOW!
You say you're a screenwriter? Great! But it doesn't always *feel* great. Why being "all typed out" and "hitting the wall" are just the start of your greatest creative breakthroughs, and why you must "strike back!"

1   CHAPTER 1:
WOW! WHAT A BAD IDEA!
How come no one is responding to your movie pitch? Why "too plain," "too complicated," and "hiding the ball" may be fatal. Plus: Fresh from the *Cat!* lab, the Rx for logy loglines and the end of the logline log jam!

21   CHAPTER 2:
IN TROUBLE IN THE CLASSROOM
So you've got the pitch down, where's the story? Step into a *Save the Cat!* workshop for new ways to "beat it out," including the "Double Bump" and e-z solutions to "Spidering," "Half-Stepping," and "Blurry Beats."

43   CHAPTER 3:
ALL LAID OUT... AND NOWHERE TO GO
Feelin' "formulaic"? Supercharge your storyline with the new "*STC!* Structure Map," including insight into "The Magical Midpoint," why "Bad Guys *Really* Close In," plus Blake's new "Five-Point Finale."

65 CHAPTER 4:
STRAIGHTENING YOUR SPINE
The script's done, but your story is off track. Why? Blake cracks open his writer's casebook to reveal the cure for "story scoliosis" and the "Five Key Questions" you need to answer to make sure you deliver the goods.

85 CHAPTER 5:
REWRITE HELL!
Going from the private to the public, now you're getting feedback... and a deadline to fix your script! Blake turns to his own *Cat!* Writers Group for answers on "How to Hear Notes" and face down problematic producers and executives.

109 CHAPTER 6:
CLOSE ENCOUNTERS OF THE SELLING KIND
Blake lets loose with hits and misses of selling — and why "The Agent Will Appear!" Plus tips that explain once and for all how to dress, pitch, and follow up on any meeting for maximum impact.

131 CHAPTER 7:
STRIKE BACK U.
Need advice over the long haul? Blake reveals secrets learned at the school of hard knocks and provides the success stories to give you winning strategies to not just survive — but thrive! — at any stage of your career.

153 CHAPTER 8:
DISCIPLINE, FOCUS, AND POSITIVE ENERGY
What does it take to succeed? What is required to elude the *real* "Dark Night of the Soul"? One man's journey to find the method to dare to dream — and win!! — in and out of the confines of Hollywood.

169 GLOSSARY

Final Terms of Engagement from the Land of the 310 — all new favorite phrases for use in the trenches, including "The Shard of Glass," "Double Dipping," and everyone's favorite, "The Smell of the Rain on the Road at Dawn."

177 ABOUT THE AUTHOR

179 REMEMBERING BLAKE

BLAKE SNYDER
OCTOBER 3, 1957 – AUGUST 4, 2009

FOREWORD

Of course, one can't help but begin this foreword with some sort of reference to franchises.

If you're reading this book, you are most likely painfully aware that Hollywood is constantly in search of the perfect, key movie element that connects so well with people and manages to be so relatable and resonant that it leaves the audience wanting more. Discovering the magic formula that creates a movie franchise is tougher than it seems — for every *Batman*, there's an *Electra* — which means a celebration is in order when a filmmaker has successfully cracked the ever-elusive code.

I'm fairly certain that when Blake Snyder started writing his first *STC!* book, the notion of being at the forefront of creating a "screenwriting how-to franchise" hadn't crossed his mind. And if it had — he was a crafty guy, after all — I imagine the idea seemed as far away and inconceivable as Indiana Jones actually finding the Holy Grail.

Yet, here we are.

Before he passed away, Blake heard from so many of his fans, all telling him he had *absolutely* cracked the elusive code! This outpouring of praise from you encouraged him to press on in his quest. With *Save the Cat! Strikes Back*, Blake — as with any good franchise creator — brilliantly found his way to a completely fresh, chock-full-of-new-material, third book in a series. Amazing. George Lucas and Steven Spielberg should take notice!

So let's take a moment to toast what Blake has accomplished in this third go 'round.

First, inspired by the workshops and lectures he'd held all over the world, Blake realized his audience wanted more — more guidance, more tough love, more common-sense advice on navigating and surviving Hollywood. He had his own experiences and anecdotes, to be sure, but he also spent the last few years *listening*. He heard thousands of questions and stories and woes from you, his loyal readers and students, and now he found the time to officially address them! So answers and reassurances to common screenwriting problems and random "what ifs" that plague rookie writers are in this book.

Next, he realized many aspiring screenwriters were having great success from the tips and the lessons presented in his first two books and, with their well-received scripts in hand, they were looking for information about "what next?" So from personal insights about agents and managers to getting and interpreting notes and what to expect in meetings, that information is in here as well.

But Blake also realized that with artistic success comes great pressure — screenwriting is a terrifying and exhausting chore on some days, an amazing but challenging career on others — so he gathered crazy tales and helpful advice from working, professional writers that present a realistic but uplifting look at the journey that is "life as a writer."

That's in here too.

And, most importantly, Blake shares a powerful, heartfelt, and intimate story of the journey that took him from a guy who had lost his creative spirit, had stopped writing and was incredibly lost, to a disciplined, positive, and driven man with a newfound desire to write, write, write. The key to his massive paradigm shift? Blake realized his stubborn, selfish, independent streak was completely ruining whatever positive mojo he might have had, so he dug down deep, reconnected with himself, and began writing from the heart. He started believing in himself again, and hopefully, his story will help you do the same.

With every word it is clear Blake wrote this book because he wanted you to know that when you decide you hate the story you're working on, when you think you've completely wasted the last six months of your weekends and free time, when you realize there's something off in your plot but can't figure out what, that **you are not alone!**

He goes out of his way to assure you, if you know in your heart of hearts you want to be a writer, there are many, many preventative and positive ways out of your screenwriting black hole. He wanted you to know he understood the struggle of a creative, inventive soul — that he and his friends had been there, for the highs and the lows of pursuing a non-traditional career path.

And that, in the end, it is all worth it.

To quote the first *Save the Cat!*: This book gives me "the same, only different." You have the same witty, wise, and kindhearted Blake, with his years of experience and positive outlook, covering a wealth of information that hasn't been touched in any other screenwriting books on the market. Blake's incredible knowledge of both the art and the business of Hollywood is only eclipsed by his infectious, passionate desire to share this knowledge with anyone looking for guidance. I'm so pleased he was able to get all this amazing, inspirational work down on paper before he died.

I wish I could congratulate him in person, but I think he already knew the importance of the legacy he was leaving. This is the stuff that franchises are made of.

No wonder readers were clamoring for more!

We'll miss you, Blake!

Sheila Hanahan Taylor
Autumn 2009

Sheila is a producer and partner of Practical Pictures, known for such movie franchises as *American Pie*, *Final Destination*, and *Cats & Dogs*. She is also a visiting professor and lecturer at various film programs around the globe, including The Sorbonne, UCLA, Cal State, Tokyo International Film Festival, and Cinestory.

INTRODUCTION: OH, YOU'RE IN TROUBLE NOW!

Let's face it, if you have chosen a career as a screenwriter, you're asking for a certain amount of pain.

A hint of this happens right up front.

No matter where you come from, what your good intentions are, or how talented you may be, when you even tell someone about the screenplay you're working on, you will invariably get looks.

Just saying "I'm a screenwriter" begs for an "Oh *yeah?!*"

And the question we all hate:

"Is there anything you've written I might have seen?"

The implication here is that if you were any good at this, you would already have something sold and made and playing at the Cineplex. And no, telling Aunt Fern about your YouTube short, or the option by the producer who almost had something premiere at a film festival *near* Sundance two years ago, is not enough.

And that hurts.

If you're like the rest of us who have picked screenwriting as your profession, you get used to it. You must — because you have to. It is *who* you are. It is *what* you are. Like Lee Strasberg as Mafiosi Hyman Roth says between coughing fits in *Godfather 2*:

"This... is the business... we have chosen."

And p.s. ta hell wid Aunt Fern.

She can barely write her name.

And she smells like cabbage.

That's right, just by checking the box marked "creative" in the list of skills you hope to turn into a profession, you are already in the trouble zone. And it's not just your concerned loved ones who stand in judgment of the ideas popping in your brain. The entire world at times seems like it's against you.

Why?

Partly because we're just different.

"They" do not get the adrenaline charge we get when we see that a re-struck print of Charlie Chaplin's *City Lights* is playing downtown; "they" do not understand the economic sense behind signing up for the 16 movies per month plan on Netflix; their minds do not flood with quite the same images as our minds do when we hear the words: "Interior, Café, Naples, 1953."

They are thinking about other things.

Cabbage, for instance.

It's like that skit I saw years ago on *Saturday Night Live*. Bill Murray is Og, the leader of a group of cavemen, strong and dumb as dirt. Steve Martin is the smart caveman, with ideas that might save the tribe. So when Steve goes to sleep by the fire, Bill picks up a rock and crushes Steve's skull, then announces:

"Now Og smart."

Yup.

Those guys.

They don't mean it personally.

They're just waiting for us to go to sleep so they can crush our skulls with a rock — because that's what they do.

And God bless 'em!

They need us, and here's a secret... we need them, too!

And yet... the *real* pain starts when something else happens.

We're going along minding our own business, being creative, running downtown to see *City Lights*, avoiding falling asleep by the fire just in case... and then one day something goes wrong.

The script we spent months on gets rejected.

The idea we thought was brilliant draws blank stares.

The empty space in the finale of our story we thought we'd know how to fill in when we got there isn't filling in.

In fact, the whole caboodle may suck big time.

And that's when the panic sets in.

The icy flush of flop sweat races down our backs.

And a horrible thought creeps into our minds:

Maybe Aunt Fern is right!?

You know what I mean. The real trouble starts not with what others think about us, but what we think about ourselves. The default position most writers have is: "I'm secretly not good at this!" And that is, indeed, not good; that will make us crazy. It takes us away from what we need to do to make it right.

We have to avoid panic, doubt, and self-recrimination.

And just fix it.

We have to get up off the mat... and strike back!

For a while now since writing both *Save the Cat!* and *Save the Cat! Goes to the Movies*, I've wanted to address that moment, the "dark night of the script" when it's just you looking into the black maw of nothingness to find your courage... and an answer. Since penning my first two *Cat!* tomes, I've had the privilege of traveling the globe teaching my method, and I've seen firsthand the looks on writers' faces when I am the bearer of bad news — or at least the bearer of news that feels bad. There is nothing worse than when ideas won't work, when structure fails, when your career looks like a wasteland, or when the panic is so great all you can think about is finally checking out those late-night commercials to be a Doctor's Assistant.

And btw, where *is* the University of Phoenix?

It's not actually *in* Phoenix.

I checked.

What I want is to give you the tools to get you back up on your horse and ride like the wind like you're supposed to — every step of the way. And I'll tell you something else, the real truth of it, and what's always given me the most hope:

Trouble is good.

If you breeze through your script or through your career without trouble, you are doing something wrong. If you are looking at trouble as a dead end instead of a learning opportunity, like some horrible curse you have to remove — instead of the gift that it is — you will never know the joys of real victory.

Every script has to have a "dark night of the script."

Every career, too.

And the fact is it's only when we hit bottom, in a script or in life, that we really prove who we are. When we decide to not give up but strike back, and do so smartly, there is a clear-headed resolve that gives us a new outlook and new determination that not only solves the problem, but also makes us the steely pros we need to be. And it gives us the experience that we can one day pass on to others who find themselves in a similar circumstance.

This book is all about that challenge. The challenge we accept from the first time we raise our hand and say "I'm a writer" (which I did at age 10 at Camp Lorr and still can't really explain why), and all the challenges along the way that are the turning points in our careers and in our characters.

It is my hope that at the end of reading this book, you, too, will look on trouble as anything but a bad thing. You will welcome "hitting the wall," "taking it as far as you can," "being all typed out," "having no new ideas," and all the other lame-ass excuses you've either heard writers give or given yourself.

That's over.

Trouble?

I laugh at trouble!

Ha, ha.

See?

And soon you'll laugh at trouble, too.

No, it's not you. It's not your talent. It's not your inability to "get it" or your "not being cut out for this racket."

It's nothing more than writing problems that need to get fixed.

If you're ready to stop your whining — *boohoo! I know Aunt Fern, yeah, yeah* — and get on with it, I'd like to quote my friend Bill Fishman's movie *Tapeheads*, starring John Cusack and Tim Robbins, and what may be the greatest line ever written:

"Let's get into trouble, baby!"

That is more than our motto. That is our battle cry.
So get ready to face trouble like a pro.
And get ready… to strike back!

chapter 1

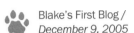

Blake's First Blog /
December 9, 2005

"By helping you win, I win too. We all do. And that is the only way to become not only a better writer, but to make the world a better place."

WOW! WHAT A BAD IDEA!

I thought I had a winner.

My book, *Save the Cat!*, had just come out. I was doing a lot of radio and magazine interviews. And my words of wisdom for screenwriters were catching on. So when a very nice reporter from National Public Radio asked if I was working on a screenplay, I told her that I was, but when pressed to say something about it, I kept mum. I'd just gotten through telling her the key thing to do if a screenwriter has an idea is to pitch it, to get reaction.

And yet here I was: a clam.

To be honest, I felt my incredible idea was *so* incredible I feared someone listening to NPR might steal it. What was worse, I was just about to start writing this work of genius and I didn't want to disrupt my creative *moojoo*. I had broken another cardinal rule I tell writers about: I was going to forgo all that "working out the beats stuff." I'd decided I was going to write "Fade In," jump on my steed, and head for the high country. And why not? I was not only a veteran screenwriter with multiple sales under my belt, I was the author of a how-to book on the subject!

A best-selling author, I might add.

You're probably ahead of me: My script never got off the ground. After stalling my manager with promises I was working on "the one," I agreed to share my idea before I started writing, and it's funny, because as soon as the words formed on my lips — the moment my thoughts took shape there in the ether above our heads — I knew I was in trouble.

The logline for my can't-miss, perfect movie?

TWINKLE — Bereft by the death of his wife, Santa Claus has 48 hours to go to New York City, find love, and save Xmas.

Don't say it!

Everyone else did.

Did I know, asked my manager, that Tim Allen already did *Santa Clause 2*? The *right* way! Did I see any problem starting my nice family film with Mrs. Claus, one of the most beloved figures in all of literature, lying dead in a snowy graveyard up at the North Pole? And what, pray tell, were we going to do about the fact Santa Claus is a jolly, 600-year-old fat man? "Oh that's easy," I said. "He can go through a magic machine that will turn him into Tom Hanks for 48 hours. That way he can fall in love with someone like Annette Bening. I have it all worked out!"

"And when Tom turns *back* into Santa Claus at the end? Will Annette get turned into a jolly, 600-year-old fat *woman*?"

My manager and I just kind of stared at each other.

"Great title though," I said to break the chill.

What no one was saying was suddenly clear:

Wow! What a bad idea!

I bring this up not to tell on myself, or even to judge what's good or bad, but to identify the indicating psychological features attached to the creation, and nurturing, of a stinker. Something about the whole process was suspicious, but there were indicators I chose to ignore — it turns out, to my peril.

The Seven Warning Signs I Might Have a Bad Idea:
- ▸ Fear of telling anyone about it
- ▸ Fear it might be stolen (by NPR listeners, no less)
- ▸ Fear that saying it out loud might spoil the "magic"
- ▸ Fear that if I don't write it fast, I'll lose it
- ▸ Lack of basic logic points — which I ignore!
- ▸ Lots of great "scenes," but no story
- ▸ Not researching to see if someone already did this

I had committed every one.

Yes, some day, in some way, Santa may get lucky. But for now, *Twinkle* is in my drawer. And that's part of the moral of the story, too: *Twinkle* might have been saved. It could have gotten worked out. But by keeping it to myself, by not involving others in my "process" like I usually do, by demonstrating gobs of hubris about my skills as a story-teller, I wrecked it.

And you do this, too. How do I know?

Because you're a writer....

"And I *dig* that about you!"

Did I commit hari-kari when I learned my idea was a non-starter? Did I cry? Stamp my foot? Throw a hissy fit?

Of course.

But when it was over I did what I always do with ideas that are yet to... gel. I went to Staples to buy more yellow pads, and started from the top.

That's also what we steely pros do.

We put a nice raw steak on that black eye, and we try again.

FADE IN: A DARK AND STORMY NIGHT

Getting through the exquisite pain of whether or not we have a good idea for a movie begins by being able to state that idea. I may not have had a sale in *Twinkle* (Jeesh, what was I thinking?), but when it came time to confess, I at least knew how to tell the tale to my manager. After years of working as a screenwriter, and knowing what lights up the eyes of my agents and others, I had condensed my story into a form that anyone could understand.

That can't be said of every writer.

Pro, amateur, or in between, we scribes find amazing ways to mislead ourselves and slip the surly bonds of practicality.

One of the inspirations for writing *Save the Cat!* was a visit to a friend of mine, a successful Disney writer with many sales and assignments to his credit. I had just stopped by to say "hi" and catch up, and then made the mistake of asking: "Watcha working on?", whereupon he excitedly said those two horrible words no one in or out of the business ever wants to hear:

"Sit down!"

I sat.

"Fade in," he began. "A dark and stormy night..." (I'm not kidding.) And 20 minutes later, he was still pitching. Scene followed tortured scene, and yes the story was logical — to a point. But the reason he couldn't tell me what his story was about was the fact that he didn't *have* a story. He too had tricked himself into thinking he didn't need to take the first step and get permission from a listener who "got it."

He'd said: "It's different this time. This is special."

Whether it's an idea we cling to that doesn't work, or scene after scene that we spill out onto the page, we are forever falling in love with ourselves, and our inspiration. I call it **The Smell of the Rain on the Road at Dawn**, that flash of scent, sight, and sound that makes us think we're onto something — and we might well be! It's the very best reason to be a writer, to find meaning where others don't, to see things the rest of the world can't. It charges our lives with a sense of the divine. It tells us that, yes, in fact we are special — we are at least especially sensitive. But unless we can figure out a way to forge that gossamer into something that makes sense to others...

We are the only ones who will ever know.

All I know is when my pal put that stinker away in *his* drawer, after writing about 50 pages of it, he called me up to complain: "Why didn't you stop me?" I will give him this: At least he had a lot more pages than I had, which is nice.

But together we were still 0 for 2.

And 0 for 2 is the kind of trouble I want to avoid.

THE PITCH VS. THE LOGLINE

How do we get our ideas across? The answer is simple: pithily. From the initial inspiration in our brain, from that first moment we sit up in bed and say "I got it!" and scramble to find a pen and try to get down what "it" is, we are looking for a way to shape that flash of brilliance into a sentence or two.

And we must!

You will get many different opinions on this, but there are two ways to describe the movie idea in our imaginations. One is to come up with a **pitch**; the second is to formalize that pitch into a **logline**. What's the difference? Well, here's my take:

The "pitch" to me is the most sales-y way to say it.

It is the most concise, easiest-to-see, fastest-to-be-able-to-tell version that still captures the crux of what it is.

Yes, pitches are hard, but essential.

For want of a better term, the pitch is best seen as **the elevator pitch**, so called because when I get into an elevator with Jerry Bruckheimer, producer of *Pirates of the Caribbean* and *CSI*, and Jerry says: "Hey Blake, watcha working on?" I don't want to have to pull the EMERGENCY STOP and say to poor Jerry:

"Fade in! A dark and stormy night!"

You have two, maybe three, floors to make an impression.

There you are. And there's Jerry. So say something!

And make it short and sweet.

One of my best pitches is for a movie I sold in 2006 called *Granny*. It sold primarily because my co-writer, David Stephens, and I delivered on the premise, but the pitch can't be denied. And though it took time to hone it down to this, it never fails. So if I ever find myself in an elevator with Jerry Bruckheimer and he asks about my latest film, I won't hesitate, I'll say:

"*Granny* is a PG-13 horror movie. It's about a senior serial killer who kills teenagers who violate the rules of etiquette. And here's the poster line, Jerry: Granny. She's off her rocker."

DING!

Jerry may not like that movie. I doubt it's one he would make, or even be interested in seeing. But he knows what it is.

And he found out in two floors.

In truth, there is no elevator, no mythic moment where it's just you and a higher-up who can change your life with 30 seconds worth of... "You're on!" But pitching is an important skill. Because at some point an audience must also be lured into seeing *Granny*, and has about the same time to figure out what it is. So the fact I can tell Jerry is good. It means Jerry can tell you...

Eventually.

As indicated, the rule on the pitch is: It's the fastest way to say it. As far as I'm concerned, anything is fair game. The best pitches include a title that tells us everything we need to know — talk about the fewest number of words! But check out:

The 40-Year-Old Virgin
Snakes on a Plane
Legally Blonde
Jaws

Each of these titles pretty much says it.

And saying it fast, grabbing us in a primal way, being a good communicator, is what you want to accomplish — for doing this work up front helps everything else that follows.

I still think it's even fair game to say: "It's reverse *Big*," the pitch that I heard from writer Robert Henny for a movie he called *Pee-Wee*, which he went on to option. I also think "It's *Fargo* in the Southwest" helps explain the 2007 Best Picture *No Country for Old Men*, because the title really doesn't.

If this feels too "sales-y" to you, too Hollywood, too artificial for your sensibilities, I hear ya, brother! But I look at it more like a service, and that takes the sting out. Part of communication is the simple idea of putting yourself in the place of the person who *isn't* in your head, who doesn't get The Smell of the Rain on the Road at Dawn. That's just good manners.

And you know how I feel about good manners.

The "logline" is the next step up, and it's a different mind-set completely. This is the formal one-or-two sentence sketch that tells us, in brief, what the story is. You may be lured by the pitch for *Granny* when you hear it, but does it say enough?

Well, that's why we need the logline.

Granny is really about Amber, a 16-year-old high school girl whose mother has just died. Her widowed father has his own troubles, her asthmatic brother his, and the girls at her school are putting pressure on Amber to go over to the dark side of sex and drugs. So when a woman claiming to be her mom's estranged mother appears at her door... Amber lets the crazy lady in.

What's the logline that says all that?

GRANNY — Saddened by her mother's death, a lonely teen must confront a woman claiming to be her grandmother, whose strict rules lead to a psychotic murder spree.

From this simple sentence an entire plot springs forth. A hero we are rooting for, an implied "transformation" she will undergo in the course of this adventure, irony galore, and a life-or-death conflict are inherent in this mini-story.

And I said it all in one line.

I flirt with you with my pitch for *Granny*, and eventually I must deliver the goods, both in the logline and in the script. But it is from this little acorn, which takes time to work out, that a glorious oak of a movie blooms. Often the pitch is easier — and easily misleading — and that's why we must nail the logline, too — a process that leads to its own trouble...

TOO PLAIN, TOO COMPLICATED, AND HIDING THE BALL

We've all had that flash of joy, that OMG! when a great concept falls into our laps from the sky. It's like finding money in the street. But eventually we have to take a moment.

And calmly, patiently, claim it.

I put my email address into both my books and on my website *www.blakesnyder.com* for that very purpose. And I get a lot of loglines. It's the I-Found-Money-in-the-Street-Can-I-Keep-It? Hotline. It's like the *Antiques Roadshow* series on TV where people bring things they discovered in their attics to an expert and he tells them if what they have is a cute little *chotchke* best left dusty, or a treasure that belongs in the Smithsonian.

I get chills when a story grabs me. Even the ones that don't can be inspiring. Oddly, these tend to fall into three categories. They are either: **Too Plain**, **Too Complicated**, or my favorite... **Hiding the Ball**.

As proof, these three slightly reconstituted (but not much) loglines I received via email show what I mean:

QUICKIE – An up-and-coming banker, engaged to his boss's daughter, goes on a stag weekend in Las Vegas, and in a drunken haze marries a penniless waitress.

PARTLY CLOUDY – A bored TV weatherman signs up for reverse 911 emergency notification service — and trouble — when it begins to micromanage all aspects of his life.

DARK STREETS – A veteran detective is on the trail of a serial killer whose identity challenges the detective's belief in the law — and the supernatural.

Let's start with the fact that I'm proud of all three of these writers. They have done the job, and I applaud them. There are stories here and they've "said it" succinctly. Each gave us:

- a *type* of protagonist
- a *type* of antagonist
- a conflict and...
- an open-ended question (what will happen?)

Not only are the form, information, and rhythm of these sentences right on, they're each *kinda* close to grabbing me. They even hit on the other key needs of a good logline:

- irony
- a mental picture that blooms in our minds
- a sense of audience and cost, and...
- a title that "says what it is"

Yet each of these, in different ways, falls short. You probably get that sense, too, but remember The Smell of the Rain on the Road at Dawn? These writers are right in the thick of it, road dust filling their nostrils, the sun just breaking on the horizon. So let's see if we can help them see it from our POV.

The first logline is a great example of what I mean when an idea is "too plain." *Quickie* is comedic and we get what's going on. But that's about all we get. Yes, there is a situation. Yes, it has possibilities. But there is an overwhelming urge on my part when I hear it to say: "So what?" What about this logline is unique? What about it is compelling me to run, not walk, to my local Octoplex?

And if you say, well, it will be different when you read the script... no. Scarily enough, whenever I read scripts that come from these loglines, it's more often than not the same experience. Since it all starts with the idea, if your logline is too plain, odds are your script will be, too. Yes, there's a story here, and yes, it has the prerequisites of drama, but it's kind of dull. This is especially apparent with *Quickie* in light of *The Hangover*, in which marrying the wrong girl is just one of *six* problems faced by the best men who have lost the groom in Vegas.

Too plain.

The second logline is a great example of "too complicated," which usually starts with confusion. I was pitched *Partly Cloudy* by a good friend, a writer who has more winning concepts than most people I know, and I apologize for picking on him with this one because 9 out of 10 of his ideas are home runs. But this leaped out at me as a perfect example of how easily we go crazy at our keyboards. When he pitched this idea via email, I smiled. It seems like a fun comedy; there's a sense of comic chaos anyway. Can you spot the problem? It should be fairly obvious.

What's "reverse 911"?

You may know, but not everyone does, and if I don't, I won't be interested. And so, still smiling, I emailed this writer back with that very question. His response made it even worse! He explained that reverse 911 is "a service you can sign up for and get alerts sent to your phone. My idea riffs off of that."

Okay, so far so good.

But then he went on to say, "The hero of my story gets phone alerts, then signs on for the optional chip implant..." Huh? Well, now I'm *really* confused. Not only am I on shaky ground with the technology he's pitching, but he's adding in something fantastic that throws me off even more.

But the real problem here is: By getting so involved with the "thing," the device that sets this story into motion, my pal completely lost the human part. How does any of this relate to a caveman like me? How's this affect the hero? What's it *about*?

Again, good thinking! This writer has an eye for ideas. But...

Too complicated.

This leads to what the third idea has wrong with it, and the concept of "hiding the ball." I love this final example because it's not just we spec screenwriters who have to confront this problem, moviemakers have to deal with it all the time.

And it costs a lot of money when we make a mistake.

Hiding the ball is really the psychological quirk writers demonstrate when they have a "secret" or a big reveal in their story. What they've got is such a whammy, such a *Sixth Sense* boffo element, they don't want to tell us about it for fear of ruining the "surprise."

But it leads to our not caring.

That's what happened to the writer of *Dark Streets*. When I got this email, I wrote back saying "too plain." There is nothing about this idea I couldn't see on an average episode of *Law & Order*. Well, she wrote back, it's because she didn't want to "give it away." *Give what away?* Well, about the reincarnation story. *The what?* It took six emails to drag the real story out of this writer, and each time, she still didn't want to tell me the secret — that it's really about a cop who discovers the killer he's chasing is... himself. There's a lot of mumbo jumbo I won't go into, but the bottom line is, even when pressed, she held back from saying it! She didn't want to ruin "the best part."

Well, I've got news: I will not ask to see that script based on what she gave me, so she'd better figure out a way to say it.

She was being too cute by half. She was hiding the ball.

And I encouraged her not to. If it's about reincarnation, tell me! If the cop is the killer, then at least give us a hint!

I love this dilemma because it even happens to the pros.

The Island is my favorite example of orb obfuscation. This is the film that came out in the summer of 2005. Directed by Michael Bay, the studio spent $150 million to make it, and another $50 million on advertising. Here in Los Angeles, there is a giant storage building near Santa Monica and La Brea and the whole face of the superstructure was devoted to the pulchritude of the movie's star, Scarlett Johansson. It is a poster one might see on the side of the Pyramids or The Hanging Gardens of Babylon. I dream about it late at night. Still!

They just had one small problem: The filmmakers couldn't tell us what *The Island* was about. And the title sure didn't help! (Is this about castaways? Is Dr. Moreau involved?) And as a result, it brought in just $35 million at the box office.

What went wrong?

The problem was the story was a secret. It's about clones who discover they're being used as spare parts for their "real," other selves. It's "*Logan's Run* with organ donors." But they couldn't say that because they didn't want to "give it away."

In my opinion, I think the movie would have done a whole lot better if they had given us a clue about the plot. If I knew going in that our heroes were being used like this, and had to run for their lives to escape being put under the knife, you've grabbed me — and even knowing this, I still don't know what happens, so I've got a reason to find out!

But the makers of *The Island* chose to hide the ball.

OTHER THINGS THAT CAN GO "WRONG" WITH AN IDEA

When pitching me, or anyone, your job is to identify the best part of your movie idea and push it to the forefront. There are other things that stop us from getting what you're saying:

▶ *Tone* - "Is it a comedy or a drama?" If I ask this, if I can't tell whether to laugh or cry, you are not communicating.

▶ *One Joke* - Your idea, while interesting, is limited. If I can't see where it goes beyond the gimmick, I won't ask for more.

▶ *No Stakes* - One cause of me saying "Who cares?" is there isn't enough on the line for the hero. I have to sense importance.

▶ *"What does the giant eat up there?"* - This line came from an agent who heard Colby Carr's and my pitch for a *Jack in the Beanstalk* update, and he was right! Any logic flaw in your pitch is fatal and stops us all from "seeing" it.

▶ *"Heaven" movies* - This goes for "Angel" movies, "one-last-chance-to-make-good-on-earth" movies, and movies where we go into "the future" or "a fantasy world." We can't root for dead people is one problem; the other is not knowing what your "world" is.

If you try to assuage me because "It's like *The Chronicles of Narnia!*", I'll tell you:

    a. Write a beloved international bestseller

    b. Sell the rights to the movies.

Then I'll buy *you* lunch.

THE END OF THE LOGLINE LOGJAM!

The way out of this conceptual miasma — and the exercise that will help you take the next step in turning your glimmer of an idea into a full-fledged script — has been created by our own José Silerio, my Development Director and right-hand man when it comes to script consultations. José took the basics of the *Cat!* method, including key points of the "Blake Snyder Beat Sheet" (which, if you haven't read my first two books, we'll discuss in Chapter 2), and put them into a single sentence for anyone who wants a little more *oomph* in his logline. And though it is no substitute for the simple pitch I prefer when I first hear your idea, it's a great way to take your idea-vetting process to the next level.

I still want to be pitched in one sentence, and I prefer the pithiest, easiest, way to say it. But if you have an idea that's not working, or if yours is too plain, too complicated, or hiding the ball, by plugging your story elements into this template, you will quickly see where you're coming up short — or why your idea might be a non-starter!

The template:

On the verge of a **Stasis = Death moment**, a **flawed protagonist Breaks into Two**; but when the **Midpoint** *happens*, *he/she* must *learn* the **Theme Stated**, before **All Is Lost**.

What do each of these phrases mean?

Let's start with "On the verge of." It's one of my favorite logline boosters. "On the verge of" describes where a hero is when we begin the story; often he's going in a very different direction from where he ends up. This handy phrase also sets up what's at stake for him.

"Stasis = Death" we will be discussing shortly, but know for now it's the moment early on when the hero suspects his life is deficient, an emotional starting point implying needed change.

Why "flawed" protagonist? Same thing. Any deficit suggests there will be a "filling in" of that flaw during the story.

What sets this story into motion? That's "Break into Two," where we see what your "poster" is — and get excited about it!

The key plot points are "Midpoint" — the "no-turning-back" part of your story — and the "All Is Lost" beat, that moment when the hero is "worse off than when this movie started." "Theme" is what your movie is "about."

And if you don't believe these simple components can be used to troubleshoot your logline, take a look at these examples:

On the verge of **another "suit and tie" assignment, a tomboy FBI agent goes undercover as a contestant in the American Miss Pageant**; but when the **pageant receives a new threat**, she must learn **to be a woman *and* tough, before she's thrown off the case and out of the bureau.** (*Miss Congeniality*)

On the verge of **returning to Earth after another routine mission, a rules-obsessed warrant officer lets an unknown alien species onto the ship**; but when **the creature kills one member of the crew and begins to grow in power**, she must **do what is right rather than what she's been told** or else **all on board will meet the same deadly fate.** (*Alien*)

On the verge of **missing Thanksgiving when his flight is diverted, an uptight ad executive is forced to travel by any means possible with a zany salesman with a secret**; but when **he loses the last rental car to get back home**, he must learn that **family is more important than his job**, and **get back in time or bust.** (*Planes, Trains & Automobiles*)

Still need more information?

Believe it or not, we can also add to this simple logline template by including **The B Story** — the love interest, mentor, or group that "helps" the hero learn the lesson — and **Catalyst**, the event that sets the story into motion, and even the **Antagonist** — our hero's nemesis or obstacle and subject to his own flaw. The enhanced template is ideal for those who have a finished script to pitch:

The enhanced template:

On the verge of a **Stasis = Death moment**, a **flawed protagonist** *has* a **Catalyst** and **Breaks Into Two** *with* the **B Story**; but when the **Midpoint** *happens*, he/she must *learn* the **Theme Stated**, before **All Is Lost**, to defeat (*or stop*) the **flawed antagonist** (*from getting away with his/her plan*).

Take a look at how these enhanced loglines tell the tale:

On the verge of **a divorce**, a **bullheaded street-smart cop** is **trapped in his wife's office building by terrorists** and **teams up with a "desk cop" patrolman to thwart them**; but when **he taunts the terrorists, and risks exposing his hostage wife's identity**, he must learn to **adapt to change** to **outsmart the leader** and stop what are really thieves **from getting away with a billion-dollar heist**. (*Die Hard*)

On the verge of **losing the girl he loves**, a **super-powered young man's abilities start to wane as a demented criminal he helped create begins to rain havoc on the city**; but when he **gives up his crime-fighting ways**, he must learn **what it means to make a promise**, before **more innocents die, to save his city from the criminal's super weapon**. (*Spider-Man 2*)

On the verge of **another meaningless year**, a **repressed high school nerd** gets **an unexpected visit from his crush** and is **left on his own under the care of his loser uncle to pursue her**; but when **enlisted by his best friend to win the student presidency**, he must **realize he has more depth than others think**, before **he loses his crush's friendship forever**, and **can finally gain his snobby peers' respect**. (*Napoleon Dynamite*)

All of these films can be found in beat sheet form either in *Save the Cat!* or *Save the Cat! Goes to the Movies*. But for fun, try using these logline templates, either the simple A Story version or its enhanced B Story cousin on any idea you have that's not working.

I think you'll be amazed by how it helps.

Juno: Can you pitch a movie that feels Indie?

JUNO: PERFECT MOVIE, PERFECT LOGLINE?

And then there was *Juno*.

I'm in the middle of putting this book together and a writer emails to say he just saw *Juno* on the plane. He almost didn't see it, even though he knew it had won the Academy Award® for Best Original Screenplay for writer Diablo Cody. Why? Because in the airplane movie guide the logline of the film read thusly:

"JUNO – A teenage girl gets pregnant."

Can you blame him?

This is a lousy logline and does not in any way reflect the experience that is *Juno* or what makes the movie special. And yet, at core, the editors of *Now Og Smart*, Caveman Airline's in-flight magazine, aren't wrong. So, if a movie with a bad logline can win an Oscar®, why should we even care? Why shouldn't we go with our gut, write "Fade In," and leave the selling to our agent?

The answer is simple.

Because nailing the pitch and the logline not only helps to sell your script — and helps you write a better story — it forces you to find its essence, the "grabber," and push it to the forefront in your pitch, so you can better deliver in the writing.

My elevator pitch for *Juno* is: "It's a 21st-century *Scarlet Letter*." I might go on to say: "It's *Baby Boom* with Doc Martens" or ask: "What if instead of saving France, Joan of Arc lived near the Mall of America and decided to have an out-of-wedlock baby?"

Have I got your interest?

Of course I do.

But what about that dreadful logline?

Although we can't control what Caveman Airlines does, when we pitch our yet-to-be-sold idea, we must do just that: sell. The email query you will write is all about a good logline. Does *Juno* have one? I posed this on my website and the winning entry came from writer Christina Ferguson:

JUNO - A plucky pregnant teen from a broken family finds herself at a crossroads between the awkward teen father and the husband of a seemingly perfect adoptive couple.

Well? I don't know about you, but I'm racing to see this movie. Christina nailed it! And she makes us realize another secret: *Juno* may be an "indie"... but it's as "high-concept" as it gets.

And if you're *still* not sure whether this idea, or any one you have, is too plain, too complicated, or hiding the ball, there's no better test than our new story template.

Here's *Juno's*:

On the verge of **another dull year of high school**, a **pregnant teen decides to have her baby and give it up for adoption**; but when **an afternoon with the would-be adoptive husband convinces her she's found the right couple**, she must learn that **some things in life can't be undone** when the **seemingly perfect couple decide to get divorced**.

Can your ideas be improved by using this method?

Totally, homeskillet.

TURN IT AROUND TO STRIKE BACK!

Are you excited?

Say "yes."

Good! You should be. Because what we've been discussing relates directly to you. If you have cringed while reading this chapter, excellent! Me too! Those "mistakes"? I've committed every one. But one thing that's been revealed for sure is: We can't hide any more.

We need to talk. We need to get in the game by not being afraid to play. To strike back we must be willing to try something new, and getting rid of our fears is the first step.

In truth, no matter how you dice it, it all comes down to hiding the ball. That's what we writers do best. We keep our ideas secret, at first just sharing with our computers, and then only with a few very special friends who understand our very special ways. We're private people; these thoughts have to germinate! We can't say it before we ourselves have a grasp of it. We can't speak it aloud until we're satisfied it's safe to share. To which I now say:

Poppycock!

Or the millennial equivalent thereof.

At the outset of this chapter, I posed the "Seven Warning Signs" that what you are working on doesn't work. Since we now have insight to fix all that, it's old news. "All stories are about transformation" and that includes the death of old ideas. So let me introduce our new creed when it comes to our pitches and loglines — and the business of spinning gossamer into gold:

The Seven Warning Signs I Might Have a Great Idea:

- ▶ I love talking about my story; I'm eager to share what I'm working on and get reaction to it.
- ▶ I have no fear my idea will be stolen! No one can tell this story like I can, and in fact someone I tell may give me an insight I didn't have before.
- ▶ I increase the magic when I say it out loud. It lets the world know I'm a writer with *lots* of great ideas.
- ▶ I can't "lose" an idea; it will only get better the more I work on it.
- ▶ I look for potential flaws in logic knowing they are an opportunity to make my story stronger.
- ▶ Even if someone wrote my story before, I can come up with a new twist that will make my version the best.
- ▶ I have a great story and that means I have great scenes — they serve my story, not detract from it!

And speaking of which, I'm not giving up on *Twinkle*. That title's not half bad and there is a way to fix the story. Maybe if we tell it from Annette Bening's character's point of view...

Yeah.

That just might work.

chapter 2

IN TROUBLE
IN THE
CLASSROOM

All over the world, since the beginning of my adventure into *Cat!*ness, I've had the pleasure of working with writers in small groups — and what a variety of locales we've met in!

In the past few years, I've led my workshops in a castle in Cornwall, England; in a beautiful farmhouse outside Barcelona, Spain; in a moldy, but evocative, old theater in Seattle; in the back of a Chicago saloon; and yes, God help us all, in the conference room of an Arizona Red Roof Inn. Sometimes in these settings it's raining outside, and the sound of a storm only stokes the imaginary campfire. For no matter where we find ourselves, when you start your pitch the only thing we hear is your story.

It's magic.

To think I almost missed out.

Teaching was not on my mind when I wrote *Save the Cat!* I said as much in its Introduction. *Dude, I have stuff to do*, was my attitude. Here's "The Last Book on Screenwriting You'll Ever Need." Good luck! And write if you get work!

Well, be careful what you don't wish for, too.

The guy who saw the promise in me, the brave soul who took a chance on a young up-and-comer, was David Lyman. I met David in Chicago during one of my early book signings and learned what an inspirational figure he is. A photographer, filmmaker, producer, and businessman, David is primarily a true "creative," who's inspired students for over 20 years at his Rockport Photographic Workshops in Maine. David asked me upon our first meeting if I'd be interested in coming to Rockport to conduct a summer class.

And never one to shrink from a challenge, I said: "Yes!"

The fear set in immediately.

On the first day of our five-day course, after my very first lecture about how the "idea" had to grab us, one student raised his hand. *Oh good*, I thought, *a question*.

"That's fine for Hollywood," the writer began, with a slight look of distaste, "but what about *good* movies?"

At which point I wondered what I'd gotten myself into.

Would you believe it if I told you that by the end of the week, he was one of my most enthusiastic supporters? And the same could be said of everyone in the class. Talk about transformation! That was the week I saw writers stretch and grow... and the week I became a teacher.

I wish for you that special day when you discover the "flow," when you look up and it's 9:00 a.m. and what seems like minutes later it's 3:00 in the afternoon. That's what happened to me. Who knew I'd love helping writers find their voices? And I've been happily doing so ever since.

But because I love story, and love trouble, the class continues to be about that other moment... the moment we disagree! You see it one way. I see it another. And you're going to have to prove your point because this is only the beginning of the pushback.

And at least I'm smiling when I say: "Try again!"

RESISTANCE IS FERTILE!

As I kept getting invited to work with writers, there was no guarantee I could continue to be effective, or that the principles of *Save the Cat!* that worked so well for my first group, and for thousands of readers individually, could be put into play everywhere.

The results have been nothing short of breathtaking!

What has developed are two separate weekend workshops for small groups of writers that do something amazing: take you from movie idea to a fully fleshed-out 40 scene outline that's ready to write.

Yet whether you attend class or not, the challenge is always the same: Can a writer hear "criticism" and respond?

I always go into these workshops knowing there will be many moments that qualify as a "throwdown." Like in my first *Cat!* group, there will come a time when one of us has to give up our old ideas and abandon everything we think we know about a story. You pitch an idea, or work out the 15 beats of your movie and think you have it down, and I'm here to say you might not. Not yet! I always want to shout:

Resistance is futile!

But I hold back.

It's a little too *Revenge of the Sith*.

Thank heaven for the group! If it were just me working one-on-one with you in that room, you might not believe me when I tell you your pitch, plot point, or theme doesn't work. There have been many times when I've stared at a writer and can tell by his silence he's digging in. But when others who are listening share my lack of enthusiasm, when "crickets" are heard, it soon begins to dawn on the writer, too. You can cling to a bad idea; you can re-pitch it six different ways, or go get a bigger hammer in hopes of pounding your story into place. But sooner or later it's clear you either have to re-think it… or let it go.

Our discussion of concept, logline, and poster that begins each class soon segues into hearing actual pitches — and the most common experience is the following:

A writer, beaming brightly, lets loose with "the one." It's why she came in; it's the idea that's sure-fire! And of course when she pitches it out, the awful silence tells all. Second pitch: same result. And that's when the panic sets in. It isn't until we prod the writer to tell us her third idea that's "nothing," the one she thought up on the way to class, that we hit pay dirt. This is what happened when Ben Frahm pitched *Dr. Sensitive* (a success story we'll be discussing in detail later in this book) or my favorite example, when a writer hit the wall in class, then out of desperation said: "I have this other thing, it's '*Private Benjamin* joins the police' and it's called *L.A.P.Diva.*"

She even had a poster line she'd been kicking around:

"You have the right to remain gorgeous!"

The booming cheers that erupted are what I remember.

AND FROM THIS LITTLE ACORN...

You can spend weeks and months massaging your logline, and should, but in our classroom we go right to the next step. And it starts with the 15 beats of the Blake Snyder Beat Sheet (the BS2), the one-page document you can print off our website that has become the go-to tool for so many.

By now, this handy template may be known to you. Since penning *Save the Cat!* I've even met writers I worked with years ago who still have a yellowed copy hanging on their wall or laminated and sitting in a top desk drawer.

If you don't know the Beat Sheet, don't worry. It's an intuitive and easy tool — and that's the point. It's the next step to start fleshing out your idea.

It looks like this:

THE BLAKE SNYDER BEAT SHEET

PROJECT TITLE:
GENRE:
DATE:

1. Opening Image (1):

2. Theme Stated (5):

3. Set-Up (1-10):

4. Catalyst (12):

5. Debate (12-25):

6. Break into Two (25):

7. B Story (30):

8. Fun and Games (30-55):

9. Midpoint (55):

10. Bad Guys Close In (55-75):

11. All Is Lost (75):

12. Dark Night of the Soul (75-85):

13. Break into Three (85):

14. Finale (85-110):

15. Final Image (110):

As I talk about the BS2 in class, and how each beat corresponds to a suggested page where it appears in an average, 110-page script, each writer is already filling in theirs, and their newly vetted concept begins to bloom. And so can yours.

What is the Opening Image and the Final Image, the "Before" and "After" that shows change in their story? What are the Midpoint and the Breaks into Act Two and Act Three? What is the "Fun and Games," the "poster" of the movie, the place where the "set-pieces" go because it's where we find the "promise of the premise"? In class — and in this chapter — I get to point out new facets of the BS2 that are only mentioned in my books.

One story element that doesn't appear on the Beat Sheet is called **Stasis = Death**, which can be found between Set-Up and Catalyst and is part of a larger conversation about "change." Stasis means "things staying the same." Death means "death." And it's the point in the story where we reveal that this hero's life isn't all it's cracked up to be — and may stay that way. After we've figured out the Set-Up and introduced all the characters in the A Story in the first 10 pages — or 10 minutes — of a movie, there is often this "sigh moment" for the hero, where we see that if things "stay the same," our poor protag is doomed.

You can see this beat in *Galaxy Quest*; it's the part where a relatively happy Tim Allen, star of a faux *Star Trek* series, overhears kids at a Comic-Con belittle and deride him. Tim snaps at fans in the next scene, and his fellow cast members worry for their "leader." But its "S=D" purpose is to show the need for change is overwhelming — and will be worth the pain of the adventure. And, of course, the most famous Stasis = Death moment is in *Star Wars* when Luke Skywalker looks at two setting suns on his home planet, and we know something's gotta give — not "next season," but now! And it sets up the Catalyst, moments later, as Luke is cleaning droids (just another day on Tatooine) when a loose screw results in a holographic Princess's plea: "Help me, Obi-Wan Kenobi. You're my only hope."

Another great Beat Sheet supercharger, and one that my class in Seattle insisted I put into this book, comes directly from this Catalyst discussion: the always-handy **Double Bump**. This doesn't have to be in every story, but often twin Catalysts are required to kick a stubborn tale into motion. In *Star Wars*, it's not enough for Luke to be summoned by a Princess; he'll need one more push that comes when he finds his aunt and uncle dead. It's the second "bump" at the end of Act One that kicks him into Two.

The Double Bump is one of many tricks to put the pieces of a story into place that comes directly from the classroom. And it points out how, when we get good at "beating it out," story problems get solved faster.

THE DARK NIGHT OF THE SCRIPT

Usually at the end of the first day of my workshop, everyone is feeling a tad brain-dead. I warn the class about this first thing. I say you will be dizzy with having your ideas shot down — and overwhelmed by other pitches. It's something I only wish on a studio executive — because that's his job. But, I also say, if you go home, have a nice meal, and get a good sleep, by the time you wake up, the birds will be singing, the sun will be shining, and the Beat Sheet Fairy will have come in the middle of the night.

And he will bring a new appreciation of how story works using the BS2. Suddenly, all those notes and suggestions that seemed so horrible the day before, so not what you wanted to do with your story, make sense, or at least start to sink in. And by the second day of class, most of the participants have a handle on their beats.

What I especially love about this class is that no matter how confusing it gets for a writer working out a story, another writer listening to your plight has a solution. Indeed, if you really take the time and push yourself, surround yourself with a writers group who will tell you the truth, then your head might explode for a day or two but in the long run your story will work.

Sometimes it's easier to see *your* blind spot in another writer's story, and many will confess as much after class: *I didn't get that I was doing the same thing as that other guy was doing... until I heard him pitch his story.*

I've stressed from the beginning the importance of the Starbucks pitch, and what you can learn from telling your story again and again, adding to it, massaging it, discovering what it really is. And the exercise of writers doing just that in our workshop proves how well this works. It's truly amazing to see a writer start with a simple "What if...", and end up with a solid, well-told tale.

That's the moment it all pays off. When your little colt of an idea struggles to its feet and stands up strong.

There's no better feeling.

And all of it is the trial and error of communication.

You *think* you're telling us, but you're not. You're certain we should get it, but we don't. But if you want to win, if you want to hit a *real* home run, you have to listen, and respond. We are like every other audience you will face from here to your Oscar® speech. There are a thousand dark nights, for a thousand different details.

You might as well get used to it.

SPIDERING, HALF-STEPPING, AND BLURRY BEATS

Some of the most frequent trouble areas that come up in class revolve around fear. A writer pitches an idea, and even creates a decent logline, but then just can't manage to take his foot off the bottom of the pool and trust that he'll actually float.

He clings to the small dream, and even wonders if he can have that. He has his idea, but he fears expanding it.

Bigger! I'm always saying.

Let's hear the story! I'm always saying.

You aren't saying what you think you're saying! I'm always saying. Yet he refuses to believe he has a winner.

Fear leads to common problems when we extrapolate from an acorn of a logline to the young sapling of a story. Hesitancy, lack of confidence — and faith — appear in three unique ways: **Spidering**, **Half-Stepping**, and **Blurry Beats**.

What are these bad habits — which you might have too?

"Spidering" occurs when a writer doesn't stick to his premise. He has a story, but is afraid of it, or afraid he won't be able to find enough story *in* it, so he starts writing a soap opera. Suddenly, all kinds of secondary tales take hold of his imagination. The hero has a brother who has an interesting problem, let's get into that! Oh! And did I tell you about his Aunt Fern and her stuffed cabbage business? Well, let's talk about that, too. Suddenly the major highway of the story expands — sideways — with errant joyrides that lead us off the main vein of the plot.

In a recent class, one wonderful writer had a blimp in his story — that had nothing to do with the plot! But by movie's end by golly, there it was... the blimp! He even had a back story for the blimp's pilot and his crew! What he didn't have was any reason to include it. From then on in class "Blimp!" became our new battle cry whenever anyone else began to stray from his story.

And trust me, we all do it!

If any of this sounds familiar, what you are doing is Spidering. You are taking the plot from the hero and giving it to minor players — and blimps — we don't care about. You're spinning webs that lead us away from the main event.

Well, don't.

One story at a time, please. It's plenty.

"Half-Stepping" is a similar delaying tactic that comes in a new form. My favorite example is what happened to a writer in my Seattle class. This writer had a sweeping historic saga, the true story of an Irish indentured servant who is brought to pre-Revolutionary America and eventually helps rally others like himself against their masters. It's "*Spartacus* in the Colonies."

So would you be surprised to learn that the writer of this amazing tale had his hero arrive in America... and do nothing?! The "Fun and Games" of the writer's early beat sheet found his protagonist in his daily duties at his master's farm. There was a scene of him plowing, a scene with the chickens, a scene where he looks around in town.

So of course I stopped the writer mid-pitch to say:

Dude!

This is *Spartacus*! And you've confined him to the world's tiniest plotline: Spartacus goes to breakfast; Spartacus takes a shower; Spartacus does some sightseeing?

This is not a story; it's an itinerary!

What this writer had fallen victim to is what I have dubbed Half-Stepping. We think we're moving the story forward with each scene, and we kinda are, but the steps are so small and insignificant, it doesn't mean much. The listener wants to grab you by the lapels and shout:

What happens?!

The writer had a stallion, and was giving us a poodle.

After having this pointed out, the writer realized his half-stepping ways had to go. By the time he came back with his pitch, it was the epic it should have been. And great!

Like Spidering, Half-Stepping shows another kind of fear and another hesitation: lack of confidence.

"Blurry Beats" is the same... but different.

This phenomenon belies the same fear, the same lack of boldness, but it is revealed not in avoiding hitting the beats, but by making them so quiet, so soft, so indefinite, we can't see them.

I find this often at the turning points of a script: the Breaks into Act Two and Three and at Midpoint. Yes, the writer kinda touches on those. And kinda hits the beats.

But I want more.

You cannot *slip* into Act Two. The Detective cannot *kinda* take the case, or suddenly *find himself* on the trail of the killer; he has to decide and step into action.

Likewise at Midpoint, the stakes can't *sorta* be raised. Big! Bold! Definite! That's how we like our plot points. And if you aren't delivering these, you aren't telling me the story. But what's really wrong is: You don't have the confidence in yourself to tell us a story that we know will work great. If only you thought so, too.

I'm your biggest fan — and I say: You can do it!

15 INTO 40

So you have your 15 beats worked out. Now what?

Well, that's easy.

In *Save the Cat!* I talk about how every movie has 40 Key Scenes and how I work out those scenes on "The Board." This simple corkboard has been the single most useful tool of my career. For those going from logline, to 15 beats, to 40 scenes, it's on The Board where it all comes together, and where we see what you've really got. But could I show writers my shortcuts to turn "15 into 40" in the classroom — and in this book?

The answer is: Yes!

For those who want an overview of what a movie is, The Board (on pages 32 and 33) is gorgeous. Please note four rows representing Act One, the first half of Act Two, the second half of Act Two, and Act Three. And look how perfectly the 15 beats fit here. But now we have to make actual scenes, 40 of them, and that begins by taking it row by row and "breaking out" key beats to flesh out the 10 scene cards per row we need.

Let's start with the first row that constitutes Act One. Take a look. If you've nailed the Beat Sheet you already have six cards out of ten: Opening Image, Theme Stated, Set-Up, Catalyst, Debate, and Break into Two.

We only need four more.

To find these, I "break out" the Set-Up card. Set-Up is where we introduce the hero and his world. You probably have a list of things you want in here to "set up" who he is. But what is the best way to organize those scenes?

Think: **at Home, at Work,** and **at Play.** "At Home, our hero lives alone; his neighbor hates him because he never takes his trashcans to the curb. "At Play," let's say our hero is into bowling, so we're going to have a scene at the lanes with his pals to set that up. While "at Work" our hero's the guy whose secretary bosses *him* around! Think H, W, and P and suddenly that one card breaks out into three actual scenes. And if you revisit at least two of these settings in your "Debate" card, suddenly your six cards become the 10 Key Scenes you need in that row. And while Home, Work, and Play don't apply to *every* story (see the Glossary for a great example of how H, W, and P appears in *Gladiator*), it's an easy way to set up "the world," and the problem-plagued hero we need to introduce.

The Board with its first 15 cards, representing each of the 15 beats.

My Screenplay - 29 Scene Cards

Save Screenplay   Title and Logline   Beat Sheet   Litter Box   Scratch Pad   New Scene Card   Verify Elements   Print

My Logline

SCENE HEADING	Card	Emotional Change	Conflict
Opening Image		+/-	><
Theme Stated		+/-	><
Set-Up HOME		+/-	><
Set-Up WORK		+/-	><
Set-Up PLAY		+/-	><
Catalyst		+/-	><
Debate HOME		+/-	><
Debate WORK	16	+/-	><
Break into Two	25	+/-	><

SCENE HEADING	Card	Emotional Change	Conflict
B Story		+/-	><
Fun and Games		+/-	><
Fun and Games		+/-	><
B Story		+/-	><
Fun and Games	42	+/-	><
Midpoint	55	+/-	><

SCENE HEADING	Card	Emotional Change	Conflict
Bad Guys Close In INTERNAL		+/-	><
Bad Guys Close In EXTERNAL		+/-	><
Bad Guys Close In INTERNAL		+/-	><
Bad Guys Close In EXTERNAL	66	+/-	><
All Is Lost	76	+/-	><
Dark Night of the Soul		+/-	><
Break into Three	85	+/-	><

Three (p. 86-110)

SCENE HEADING	Card	Emotional Change	Conflict
Finale POINT 1		+/-	><
Finale POINT 2		+/-	><
Finale POINT 3		+/-	><
Finale POINT 4		+/-	><
Finale POINT 5	95	+/-	><
Final Image	110	+/-	><

The Board with additional cards for Set-Up (at Home, Work & Play) and Debate (Home & Work) in Row 1, alternate B Story and Fun & Games cards in Row 2, alternate External and Internal scenes in Fun and Games in Row 3, and five cards for the five "Points" in the Five-Point Finale in Row 4. It's easy to add cards to your original 15!

Moving on to the second row, which represents the first half of Act Two from the Break into Two to Midpoint, we only have three cards appearing from the BS2: B Story, Fun and Games, and Midpoint. How can we get 10 cards from these? Well, again, you're farther along than you think.

What we're looking for in this row is a combination of B Story and Fun and Games as we move toward Midpoint. The B Story, which starts here, details how the hero meets the love interest, mentors, and sidekicks he'll need to "learn his lesson." How the hero is adapting to this new, weird world is the Fun and Games. By pushing the hero forward and "shuffling" B Story and Fun and Games "set pieces" — B Story-Set Piece-B Story Set Piece — 10 cards are easy. This is seen in *The Matrix* when Neo (Keanu Reeves) crosses into the "hidden world" and meets a series of B Story mentors, and learns his new skills in Fun and Games that take him from cubicle-dwelling Joe to possibly "The One" by the Midpoint — all by shuffling B Story and set-pieces.

Row #3, which represents the second half of Act Two, may seem similarly daunting but is just as easy to fill in. Having a problem with Bad Guys Close In? Can't think of enough scenes to complete that part of your story? Think **External** and **Internal**. "Externally," how is the actual "bad guy" putting pressure on your hero(e)s, and circling closer? What's the other half of that equation? Think "Internally." How is the hero's "team" reacting to this pressure, and falling apart? Alternate these two sets of scenes by thinking E and I and you'll have more than enough. By the time you hit All Is Lost, Dark Night of the Soul, and Break into Three, you'll easily get 10 cards.

And as for what happens in Row #4 and Finale, I will have more to say on that subject, but here again, 10 cards is easy! It's just a matter of finding the five essential beats that make up the "Final Exam" the hero must undergo to prove he's learned the lesson, and can apply it himself.

What's great about this method is there is always a way to check your progress. We start with an idea, break it out to a logline, break that out to 15 beats, and then 40.

And if you want to try this at home, we've created a virtual Board in our best-selling *Save the Cat!* story structure software that is available on my website.

I love it! But even if you use an actual corkboard, push pins, and index cards, that still gets me excited. For whether you use the old-fashioned type, or our electronic version, being a "Master of the Board" never fails to create the most important result:

A story that resonates.

MORE COOL STUFF

Whenever I get in front of a group of writers, I am forever worried about overloading them with information. I have this download of e-z-2-use tools I want to transfer from my brain to yours. It's only because I love my job, and love writers, that I want to push you right to that edge without going over the line. But there are times when I can see it in your eyes:

"I'm smiling, Blake, but in my brain… it's Chernobyl!"

This is why we now break the workshop into two separate units with the first weekend working out the 15 Beats and the "graduate" class, or "Board Class," dealing with the 40 cards of The Board. But that was not always the case; in the early days of these workshops, we tried to do it all from idea to 15 beats to 40 scene cards in one weekend! I worry sometimes that I'll get a call from the relatives of one of those participants to ask what their family member means by "All Is Lost" — the words they keep mumbling from their bed in the facility where they've been held since my class.

Oh well! Trial and error.

"And we're walking, we're walking…"

In addition to working out what happens in each of the 40 cards, in the Board Class we also get into both "emotional shift" (denoted by the +/- symbol on each scene card) and "conflict" (denoted by the >< symbol on the bottom of each scene card). Each of these is a separate conversation, and one you must deal with in your script.

In terms of the emotional shift (+/-), since every scene is a mini-story, each scene tracks change. Characters walk into a scene feeling one way and walk out feeling another. And while it may be too precise to show exactly what emotions those are in the planning stage, we can easily tag every scene as either positive or negative. And I encourage you to do just that. Often it's enough to say each scene is either a "+" or a "-" as it relates to Theme.

In the cataclysmic sci-fi epic *Deep Impact*, for instance, the Theme Stated question is: Will we survive the humongous comet streaking toward Earth? Each scene of the movie, believe it or not, alternates with "+" Yes we will or "-" No we won't. Yes. No. Yes. No. That's the thematic structure and the up and down of the emotional ride of that movie. My own *Blank Check* is like this, too. The Theme Stated of our family comedy about a boy who gets a million dollars is: "He who has the gold makes the rules!" Is it true? Well, scene by scene it fluctuates "+" Yes, it's true, money is fun! followed by "-" No, it's not, money isn't everything. Yes. No. Yes. No. All the way to the end.

Conflict (><) offers more challenge, especially when you're having a hard time finding it in your scenes. How many scenes have conflict in a 110-page screenplay? That's right. Every. Single. One. And yet finding that conflict in all scenes isn't easy. During an early class, the wonderful writer/actress Dorie Barton was working out cards for her L.A. thriller, *Migraine*, and we had a scene wherein the protag, a waitress hampered by severe headaches, explains to her boss what a "migraine" is. It's pure exposition, and the scene just lay there. Why? No conflict! Well, to fix that, we shoved some conflict in. We created a customer who, while the hero goes on explaining her condition, keeps banging on the counter. "Miss! More coffee over here! Miss! MISS!" The **forced conflict** of that scene makes it play better — and reinforces the pained look on the hero's face as her migraine builds.

"Forced conflict" like this appears in lots of movies. My favorite example is in the Tom Cruise racecar epic, *Days of Thunder*. It's a simple scene: NASCAR driver Tom phones doctor Nicole Kidman, whom he just met, to ask her out on a date. Very dull. Aside from the conflict of "Will Nicole say yes?" what other conflict is there? So the writers have placed this scene in the break room at Tom's workplace, where Tom's co-workers get their coffee. Since everyone is curious about Tom, they keep busting in for another cup of java — and embarrassed Tom keeps pushing them out, wanting privacy. The scene now demands attention. Forced conflict can feel phony — Tom could make the call from the pay phone across the street, right? — but we get better at it with practice. Because we must put conflict into ALL our scenes!

Dorie Barton at the Board in one of our first classes (taken with one of the first cell phone cameras).

And there is no better way to vet this, or test if your scene has conflict, than putting it up on The Board.

"DEATH" AND THE PLEDGE COMMERCIAL

Some writers are surprised to learn how many ways the beats of the BS2 can offer insight into storytelling. In fact, it can be used for any story, no matter what length or type. And yet here's a shocker for many of you:

The 15 beats can also be used to write a scene!

Did I just blow your mind?

I hope so.

To repeat, a scene is like a mini-story. Like a whole movie, it has emotional shift and conflict. It also has a Midpoint, Breaks into Act Two and Act Three, and a definite All Is Lost. It's amazing... but true. I also hold to the idea that pinpointing the All Is Lost is the key to getting your bearings. If you can't identify the beats of the scene you are writing, or watching, identifying the "death moment" about three quarters of the way in is a good place to look.

We begin every scene, like every movie, with a hero who has an expectation. He also has an obstacle: a person, a problem, a question that needs answering. And at any given point in that scene, there is a "death." In class, I dissect the scene in *Godfather 2* where Michael Corleone (Al Pacino) meets with his wife, Kay (Diane Keaton). He's just outwitted Senate investigators and wants to tell her his next move and his plans for their future together, expecting her and their children to snap to.... Well, think again, Al! After the Set-Up — Al in charge — and the Break into Two — laying out his plans — Al is surprised when Diane says: "No." That's the Midpoint "bump" of the scene.

This "raising of the stakes" is a definite turning point in Al's expectation, and the Bad Guys Close In section sees him reeling, trying to figure out what's going on. But it's the All Is Lost point and its "Whiff of Death" that solves the mystery. It's the shocking news Diane reveals to Al that her "miscarriage" wasn't. "It was an abortion, Michael!" Diane tells him. Well, not only is this a death moment of the Corleone marriage but of the scene, too. Whatever expectation Al had at the start is over.

Death is even found in a 30-second commercial that hits ALL the beats. Take a look at a story we'll call:

The Day I Discovered Pledge

Opening Image — A downcast housewife. Home a mess. Dust everywhere. This "Before" snapshot depicts the Set-Up, and even a Stasis = Death moment, for it looks like things won't change.

Catalyst — Then our hero discovers... Pledge!

Debate — "Should I use it?"

Break into Two — Yes!

Fun and Games — With a spray can of her B Story ally, the delighted homemaker flies through the house, dust vanishes like magic, tabletops glow. And the "false victory" at Midpoint shows that she can live this way all the time. But there's a problem...

Bad Guys Close In — To have the "new," she must give up the "old." Can our hero face the truth of what she must sacrifice?

All Is Lost — What "death" has to occur? What "old idea" must be gotten rid of? What is the "All Is Lost" moment of our Pledge commercial? Why it's dropping Brand X in the trash! It's the furniture polish our hero used to use, that is now obsolete.

Break into Three — Having dispensed with Brand X, the synthesized pair finish up the housework with delight and...

Final Image — Dressed in her tennis outfit, racket in hand, a newly together housewife walks out the door, leaving the primally named Pledge atop a very shiny table to guard her home.

The End

That's a lot of drama for 30 seconds!

But it's there: a transformation — a story with drama, fun, and yes, even a "death" before its final triumph!

More than that, it's proof the BS2 can be used for any story, of any length, where a narrative arc is found.

SPECIAL TROUBLE IN THE CLASSROOM

I frankly love it every time I work with writers in small groups and start hearing pitches. Out there our problems are seemingly insurmountable, but in here, wherever our classroom is, we're in charge. We can mold our stories, invent characters and situations, pitch out wild set pieces and even wilder showdowns.

And we don't have to commit to any of it.

This is sketching. Like an artist, we start with a faint idea. And as we work it out, we go from rough drawing to filled-in outline, to painting — trying out details as we go. And at any given stage, if we're any good, we can back off and say: None of it works! We can erase parts and start again, and the benefit of the *Save the Cat!* method is: We have yet to type Fade In. Our motto: Be flexible. Because that's so empowering!

What often stops empowerment from happening is the writer's unwillingness to let go — or to see his or her story in a new way. That leads to special trouble when these same old problems keep popping up. So let this be a warning to writers of the following:

▶ *"This happened to me!"* — I shudder every time someone comes in with a so-called true story. Sorry! But let me say, when I start to twitch, when I realize the hero of your pitch is... you... it hurts. Why? Because one's life seldom makes a good movie. The other reason is if there's even a slim hope we can make something of it, you are less likely to be flexible. "That's not how it happened" is your comeback, and mine is: "We don't care." You think these events are cool. You may be the only one. Story first. Reality second. Story first. How it felt second. Story first. True stories... rarely.

▶ *Copying* — I am a big believer in "give me the same thing... only different." I am against copying. Many times we will be halfway through a pitch and a vague recollection will come to me: I've heard this story somewhere before. Not kinda the same: the same. This is a direct result of a writer who has discovered a very obscure movie, and whose intention is to retell it — exactly. Usually I am pretty good at spotting this. I am the man with 10,000 plots in my head. I've seen them all — or most. But this is a non-starter. If you are taking this tack, please reconsider.

▸ *Fantasy worlds* — Again I hark back to my warnings in Chapter 1 about "Heaven" stories. I have found after a 20-year career as a screenwriter, and several years wrestling with writers in the classroom, that the single toughest story nut to crack is when you bring me a story of an original "fantasy world" the hero lives in or travels to. You may think you see it, but you don't. And when I ask simple questions like "What's the problem?" or "What are the rules?" of this new world, you often are offended. I am only trying to let you know that the specialness of your special place may be covering up the real problem: no story! To sell us on it, you'll have to work extra hard to make your fantasy real.

"IT'S EASY!"

The success stories that have come from using the method we've perfected in class are remarkable. But the biggest lesson I've gleaned from watching so many writers crack their stories is it's best to walk in the door with an idea that's just beginning to germinate. That, and flexibility — plus a willingness to listen — are key.

And being the most excitable person in that room, I often have to be contained from jumping up and down as I watch a story that was barely there blossom before my eyes.

But it happens all the time.

Recently, a writer came in with just a title and the barest semblance of a pitch, and within the first weekend had 15 beats that were ready to go. But wanting to make sure, she came back and did her 40 cards and, honestly, it got even better. It was such a great pitch, I called her afterward to tell her that what she had was pure gold.

She wrote the script in a week. And we're still waiting for it to go "out to the town." But the joy of watching that slim notion become a story is the payoff.

Because for me it's proof that the method works.

Wherever two or three are gathered, or even if you apply these principles on your own, we can all find our way out of the pitfalls, back up from any seeming dead end, get out of any jam, and find our way to the winner's circle.

So long as we remain open to new ideas.

My favorite expression in class, and one that boggles the minds of many when I say it with a big smile on my face, is:

It's easy!

You are struggling, drowning, confused, and hating it all, and I'm beaming at you, repeating this horrible phrase like I have the answers at the back of the book and won't show you!

It's easy! I say… because it is.

There is always an answer!

Within every story is the potential for not only a fix — but greatness. And I'm smiling because I not only know you can do it, but the process of doing it is so much fun — if you let it be.

Because I know magic can't be far behind.

chapter 3

ALL LAID OUT... AND NOWHERE TO GO

Blake's Blog /
August 2, 2007

"We transform every day, re-awaken to new concepts about the world around us, overcome conflict, and triumph over death... only to start again each morning. It's why stories that follow this pattern resonate. Because each day is a transformation machine, and so are our lives."

Overcoming hurdles.

That's what *Save the Cat!* is about.

Yet when it comes to the topic of "structure," which I think makes *Save the Cat!* a breakthrough for any screenwriter, the trouble I've gotten in for being a structure advocate is puzzling.

We all have deficits in our writing skills. Some of us are missing the "idea gene," some are horrible at titles, but without structure we're sunk. Yet the fights I get on this topic astound me, and lead me to believe I haven't quite made my case. The good news is: Of the skills it takes to be a great storyteller, structure is the easiest to learn — if you're open to it.

And if you are, it is also the most empowering!

I think the biggest misconception about structure, and the biggest block for many writers, is the sense that I'm asking you to do something "formulaic." Can I be honest with you, just you and me? This objection exhausts me. Let's just say for now that those who argue against structure on the basis that it is stopping you from "being free," or feel that if you follow my advice you'll be doomed to write *Big Momma's House 2* over and over, are wrong. And if you've read my second book, which applies this so-called "formula" to everything from big studio hits like *Spider-Man 2* and *Forrest Gump* to Indies like *Open Water* and *Saw*, and you *still* aren't convinced these a) hit the beats, and b) are extremely different, well... you will have trouble with structure, and that's no fun!

And yet...

I grant you there are times when having diligently followed my suggestions, and worked out your structure as I prescribe, there is unease to having it all so nice and neat. There is something about it that feels mechanical, too "clean," or too simple. And that's no good either. If you've worked out your story but haven't started writing, it may be because you've lost the reason for writing it; the inspiration's gone, you're not *feelin'* it! It might be because you know too much about your tale to be surprised when you actually put cursor to computer screen.

And if you have written a draft, you may have hit all the beats like a master, and the pieces are in place, but the emotion isn't. Your hero seems so much like an order-taking automaton that neither you, nor we, have much interest in seeing where he goes.

If any of the above applies, it feels like trouble indeed.

Whether you bridle at the idea of churning out duraflame® logs that seem so much like firewood, but aren't, or if you just plain don't get it yet, take heart. This is the chapter where we answer your structure dilemmas once and for all, so you will feel confident every time you fully flesh out any story you write.

We must start with the fact your story is not unique.

I know! I know! That sounds bad. I can see you now, in your garret, with your bowl of Top Ramen, cursing me!

But it's true.

You can break up time, as they do in *Memento* and *Pulp Fiction*; you can have anti-heroes as seen in *American Psycho* and *Election*; you can intertwine multiple stories, as in *Babel* and *Crash*; you can pull the rug out from us by saying "And then I woke up, it was all a dream!"

as exploited in *Atonement* and *Stranger Than Fiction*. Yes, you can break all the rules, with varying degrees of success, but you will never evade the principles that come by conquering structure — for until we find a way to live on Earth without lessons on how to do it, we're going to be stuck with storytelling principles all writers must master.

We're going to be stuck with structure.

THE TRANSFORMATION MACHINE

As stated in the previous chapters, all we're looking for — both as writers and as audience members — is a tale that grabs us by the gonads. Our job is simple: to be *astounding*! And doing that is actually easy... so long as we meet only one demand:

Tell us a story about transformation.

I like to say that as we begin any story, you the audience and I the writer are standing on a train platform. You and I are getting on that train... *and we're not coming back*. The tale we tell is so life-altering, both for the hero and for us, that we can never look at our world the same way again. Others may be lingering on the platform, they may talk about the trip, but in truth it's only talk; they've never actually been anywhere.

It's because change is not only astounding, it's painful.

Every story is "The Caterpillar and the Butterfly."

We start with a caterpillar living among the tall branches, eating green leaves, waving "hi!" to his caterpillar pals, little knowing that his is a life of profound deficiency. And then one day, an odd feeling comes over him that's so scary, it's like a freefall. Something strange is happening. And that something... is death. That's what the cocoon stage is. As caterpillar becomes chrysalis, he dies. He, and everything he knows, is no more. Can you imagine? But when it seems like this purgatory will never end, when things look blackest, there's another stirring; our hero sees light, and now he breaks through a weak spot in his prison, to sunlight... and freedom. And what emerges is something he never dreamed of when this all began, something... *amazing*!

That's every story.

And if you call that "formula"...

You're still on the train platform talking about it.

Because change hurts.

And only those who've had to change, and felt the pain of it, know that at a certain point it is also inevitable. It's like those *Tom and Jerry* cartoons where Jerry the mouse ties a string to Tom the cat's tail, and runs the end all over the house, then anchors it to an anvil up on the roof. With one push, the look on Tom's face tells us he knows... he's going! And there will come a moment — like it or not — when he's pulled ass-backwards through a keyhole! Overall, we'd prefer Tom to experience this sensation.

And that's why we tell stories.

There are all kinds of ways to map out this change, but never forget that's what we're charting here. We will get bored not seeing change occur. Despite all the pyrotechnics you throw our way that dazzle us so, we must experience life. And the trouble we get into as screenwriters comes when we think "The Caterpillar and the But-terfly" is too simple to apply to us.

So how do you find the transformation in *your* story?

In *Save the Cat!*, *Save the Cat! Goes to the Movies*, and chapter two of this book, I go into great detail about two different maps to chart change: the 15 beats of the Blake Snyder Beat Sheet and the 40 beats of The Board.

But in the course of teaching structure, I've found another way, a third map, that may be the easiest way to see story yet. This is the "flow chart" that shows **The Transformation Machine** that is change in action. It illustrates how, in the process of change, the hero dies and the person emerging at the other end is wholly new. We can actually track that change using this chart.

Are you ready for a little change yourself?

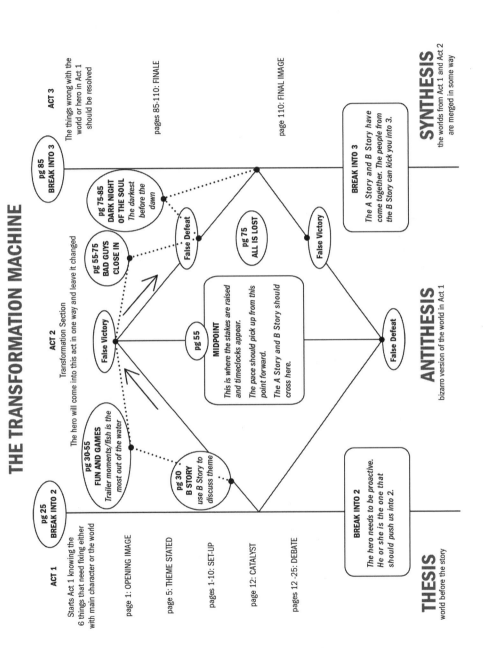

THE TRANSFORMATION MACHINE

ACT 1

Starts Act 1 knowing the 6 things that need fixing either with main character or the world

page 1: OPENING IMAGE

page 5: THEME STATED

pages 1-10: SET-UP

page 12: CATALYST

pages 12 -25: DEBATE

pg 25 BREAK INTO 2

ACT 2

Transformation Section

The hero will come into this act in one way and leave it changed

pg 30 B STORY

use B Story to discuss theme

pg 30-55 FUN AND GAMES

Trailer moments/fish is the most out of the water

False Victory

pg 55-75 BAD GUYS CLOSE IN

pg 55 MIDPOINT

This is where the stakes are raised and timeclocks appear.

The pace should pick up from this point forward.

The A Story and B Story should cross here.

False Defeat

pg 75-85 DARK NIGHT OF THE SOUL

The darkest before the dawn

pg 85 BREAK INTO 3

ACT 3

The things wrong with the world or hero in Act 1 should be resolved

pages 85-110: FINALE

pg 75 ALL IS LOST

False Victory

page 110: FINAL IMAGE

False Defeat

THESIS

world before the story

BREAK INTO 2

The hero needs to be proactive. He or she is the one that should push us into 2.

ANTITHESIS

bizarro version of the world in Act 1

SYNTHESIS

the worlds from Act 1 and Act 2 are merged in some way

BREAK INTO 3

The A Story and B Story have come together. The people from the B Story can kick you into 3.

THREE WORLDS

We start with the fact there are three different "worlds" in a well-structured story. We hear these worlds called many things, including Act One, Act Two, and Act Three, but I prefer to think of them as "Thesis," "Antithesis," and "Synthesis."

Thesis is the world "as is"; it's where we start. You as the writer have to set the world up for us and tell us its rules — even if you think they are obvious. Where we mostly get into trouble as screenwriters is discounting the need to stand in the shoes of the audience who know nothing of what's in our brilliant imaginations. We have to be considerate — and clear. What is the historic time period? What strata of society are we in? Is it fantasy- or reality-based? Who is our hero? Is he underdog or overlord? What is his burning desire? The world of *Gladiator* is different from *Blade Runner* and different again from *Elf*. When we open our eyes, what do we see, who's in charge, what are the codes of conduct? And what are this world's deficiencies?

In each of the movies cited above, there's also a systemic problem: an empire in transition, killer replicants on the loose, a human — raised by elves — who suddenly learns the truth. What we are setting up is not just a place but a dilemma. And we have to set it all up to understand where we will soon be heading.

Antithesis is the "upside-down version" of the first, and absolutely must be that. I often cite *Training Day* as an example to distinguish these worlds, for when Jake (Ethan Hawke) is given a choice at Minute 17 by Alonzo (Denzel Washington) to "take a hit off that pipe or get out of my car," and proactively says yes, Ethan leaves behind the world of "ethical" cops that is his Thesis world and enters its "funhouse-mirror reflection."

Often characters re-appear in a different form in the Antithesis. Think how Dorothy, in *The Wizard of Oz*, meets funhouse-mirror versions of characters she left back in Kansas. In *Gladiator*, Russell Crowe trades noble Marcus Aurelius (played by Richard Harris) for the moth-eaten version in the gladiator impresario played by Oliver Reed. In *Elf*, Will Ferrell leaves elves in the North Pole, who told him he was human, for humans pretending to be elves — to get a job as an elf at a NYC department store!

Part of the reason for making the Antithesis world an odd mirror reflection of the Thesis world is a simple truth: We can leave home and go somewhere else, but our problems are always with us. In *Legally Blonde*, let's face it: Elle Woods (Reese Witherspoon) is a sort of a pill when we meet her. Yes, she's put down for being blonde, but she kinda deserves the label. Going to Harvard forces her to change by setting her in a world where her flaws are obvious. But have no doubt, her problems haven't gone anywhere, and that's why characters from before manifest in different form — just as in life. It's like the person who says: "Everyone in Los Angeles is mean!" and decides to move to a new town, where he discovers that "Everybody is mean here, too!" Sooner or later, it will dawn on this person it's not the town that's the problem; it's something he's doing wrong that's causing "mean people" to always appear.

Again, good storytelling is so, because it reflects truth.

Often distinguishing these two worlds must be forced. I worked with a writer whose logline was: "A struggling artist fakes his death to raise the price of his work and hides out in the world of the homeless, only to discover his agent is actually trying to kill him." (A fear I've had for years!) Problem was: The struggling artist lived in a cold-water flat, and was already broke when we start, so when he fakes his death and hides among the homeless, what's the difference? We changed it to make the Thesis world different, and make the poor artist successful and living in a penthouse! Now the change in worlds is more drastic, richer — and as a result the story is richer, too.

The third world is a combination of the two: Synthesis. What the hero had in Thesis, and added to in Antithesis, becomes "the third way" in the finale. Again citing *Training Day*, Ethan Hawke starts out as an ethical cop in Thesis, then learns a new way in the upside-down world of dirty cops. By the time Denzel Washington tries to kill Ethan by dropping him at a gang house, Ethan, metaphorically, "dies" at the hands of the gang members. In the very next scene, Ethan has a "Dark Night of the Soul" as he rides a bus around downtown L.A. and we know he can't go back to the way he was before. The old Ethan would head to the police station and tattle on Denzel: "Teacher, teacher! Denzel did a bad thing!" But Ethan is so changed by what he's learned in Act Two, he can't go back. Like our caterpillar, the old Ethan is dead. And to emerge in Act Three victorious, he has to retain his ethics, add that to what he's learned, and become a "third thing."

These three worlds force change in a hero. We set him up, throw him in the blender, and he emerges as something brand new.

Much of the troubleshooting I do with your story is an examination of these three worlds. By looking at the process of change this way, it's easy to step back and take in the big picture of how your hero or heroes move through these phases to their final destination. What I'm always going for is: bigger — or at least clearer — ways to define **the bouncing ball** that is your protagonist and the various ups and downs he must go through. The biggest surprise for most writers is: You are the engineer here! You are "small g" god of this universe and can make it any way you want! Whenever I point out how minor the changes are in your hero, or how the overall arc is insufficient, writers are forever saying: *But that's not how I saw it*, as if the way it came out of your imagination is the only way it can be. This is why picking your Opening Image and Final Image is so vital, and why you have to keep adjusting the Alpha-Omega and make those two points as wildly opposite, and as demonstrably different, as possible.

And I know you get it because you are awesome! And I'm not just saying it because you've come with me all the way to page 50!

THE MAGICAL MIDPOINT

Given these three worlds, we can now put the 15 beats of the BS2 into the Transformation Machine and look how nicely they lay out! From left to right we see Opening Image, Theme Stated, Set-Up, Break into Two, through Midpoint, All Is Lost, Finale, and Final Image.

And each stop on our trip in some way changes the hero.

Let's start with Midpoint or what I am calling the "Magical Midpoint," for in fact it is a very magical place. When I noted in the first *Cat!* book how vital Midpoint is for "breaking" a story, I had no idea how much more I'd keep learning about it.

I like to say that the Midpoint is the Grand Central Station of plot points, the nerve center. It's because so many demands intersect here. The Midpoint clearly divides every story into two distinct halves and is the "no-turning-back" part of our adventure. We've met our hero and shown his deficiencies, we've sent him to a new place, and in Fun and Games we've given him a glimpse of what he can be — but without the obligation to be that! Now at Midpoint, we must show either a false victory or a false defeat that forces the hero to choose a course of action, and by doing so, make his death and rebirth inevitable.

False victory at Midpoint is just that, the point where the hero "gets everything he thinks he wants" — and it has features that are fascinating. Many times you'll find a "party at Midpoint": the celebration Jim Carrey is feted with in *Bruce Almighty* when he gets his promotion to anchorman, and even a "kiss from the girl"; check out *Ironman* when, fresh from the false victory of his first trial flight as a superhero, Robert Downey Jr. goes to his company party and almost kisses Gwyneth Paltrow; look at the party Dustin Hoffman attends in *Tootsie*, when he tries to fly as the man Jessica Lange might kiss, but gets slapped down by her instead. And even when there's not a party per se, there is often a "public coming out" of the hero as he tries on this new identity, or declares a new way of living. Kate Winslet and Leonardo DiCaprio do this at the Midpoint of *Titanic*, when, after making love for the first time, they go up on the deck of the soon-to-be-doomed ship together for all the world to see.

False defeat is the same but opposite. The Midpoint false defeat is where the hero "loses everything he thinks he wants." It also has a public aspect. Check out the costume party in *Legally*

Blonde, when Elle Woods bottoms out in her bunny ears and is told by ex-love Warner he doesn't want her, and that she should leave Harvard. Note the false defeat party of *Spider-Man 2* when Tobey Maguire learns Kirsten Dunst is engaged. It's the point where Richard Gere is broken in *An Officer and a Gentleman*, and — publicly — declares defeat by shouting to drill sergeant Lou Gossett Jr. his melodramatic secret: "I got nowhere else to go!"

Whether a false victory or a false defeat, the purpose of this Midpoint "public display of a hero" is to force that hero to announce himself as such — and up the ante of his growth. We've had some fun, we've seen you either rise to the top or crash spectacularly; you've tried out your new identity — here in the upside-down version of the world — but what are you, the hero, really gonna do about it? Are you real or are you fake?

"Stakes raised," "time clocks" forcing his decision, the hero must decide. What's it gonna be, pal: butterfly or worm?

The Midpoint is where the hero stands up and says: Yes, I'm going through with this. Whether by dumb luck, determination, or pressure from the "Bad Guys," he must keep going forward.

And speaking of Bad Guys, this is where they start to "close in" — and there's a good reason for that, too. Part of the risk of declaring one's self a hero is that it attracts the attention of those who most want to stop us from growing, changing, and winning. The Bad Guy/Good Guy intersection at Midpoint is key to upping the stakes of that conflict. The Midpoint is the place where "the Bad Guy learns who his rival is," as Alan Rickman does when he first meets Bruce Willis and his cowboy persona at the false victory Midpoint of *Die Hard*; it's where the secret power or flaw of a hero, or his role in besting the Bad Guy, is discovered, as in *Eternal Sunshine of the Spotless Mind* when Jim Carrey's rival for Kate Winslet's affections (Elijah Wood), learns he's getting competition from Jim... *still*; it's also where, if the hero is hiding, or his location is unknown, "the Bad Guy learns the hero's whereabouts." We see this when the chasers in *Witness* realize Harrison Ford is hiding in buttermilk country, and when Peter Coyote and his gang of key-jinglers discover E.T. is secreted somewhere in suburbia.

The Magical Midpoint has all these characteristics, but like a writer brilliantly pointed out in my workshop one weekend, it's not all *on* page 55! These beats are spread out, often over several scenes mid-way. To quote Gene Wilder in the dart-throwing scene of *Young Frankenstein*: "Nice... grouping!"

WHY BAD GUYS *REALLY* CLOSE IN

Having crossed the "point of no return" at Midpoint, a hero of a story begins the most difficult phase of his transformation.

And this is true for the writer of the tale as well.

Remember change is painful. Midpoint is not only the end of the Fun and Games and the glimpse of what a hero can be, it's the knowledge that he has to change. Whether a false victory or a false defeat, the lesson's not over. That's why the hero starts to fight it from here until All Is Lost. *I don't wanna go!* you can almost hear him cry. But like it or not, he's going!

And you as the writer have to go with him.

Part of the reason this section is so difficult to figure out is it's about stuff happening *to* the hero — that will lead to the ultimate when he "dies" on page 75. As writers we like our heroes to be proactive, leading the charge, always in control.

But this is the part where what the hero once believed was real, solid ground, is crumbling away, forcing him to react.

After the false victory beat in *Alien* when the monster attached to John Hurt's face drops off and "dies," Sigourney Weaver and the crew of the *Nostromo* prepare to go back to Earth.

Hey! Let's have a party!

But once that creature splatters John's stomach all over the dinner table and skates off squealing into the darkness, the disintegration of Sigourney's world begins in earnest. Not only do her fellow crew members start getting eaten right and left, it's slowly dawning on Sigourney that her belief in the company is false... and the rules she thought would keep her safe, won't.

And that's unthinkable.

So she resists. And resists. And resists.

Until it becomes painfully obvious at All Is Lost.

That's Bad Guys Close In. Externally, aliens are actually attacking. Internally, we are still clinging to our old beliefs.

And one by one they are being exposed as false.

Resistance is not as easy to write as proactive, leading-the-charge, directioned activity that heroes normally exhibit.

How do you reveal the internal fear of a hero, for whom it's gradually being revealed her old beliefs are wrong? How do you show panic — which most heroes are trying *not* to show?

That's why BGCI is so tough to write!

But if you know that's the purpose of that section, it's at least easier to think about, plan, and aim for in your writing. This is disintegration of the old ways, the slow sloughing off of ideas, beliefs, and friendships that are wrong, useless, harmful. The horrible realization that the keyhole is near and you're going through it and there's no escape. We... are... going!

And that realization begins at the Magical Midpoint.

THE THEME STATED – B STORY CONNECTION

Why are there so many scenes at Midpoint that involve the "hero kissing a girl," you may well ask? It's because another intersection that happens here at Midpoint is the **A and B Story cross**. And since many writers have asked for more on this, there's no time like the present for further elucidat'n'.

Midpoint is not only where we "raise the stakes" of the hero's A Story, but where we do the same for the B Story. And that's why the boy and girl so often kiss here — or at least come close. I told this "discovery" to an old-time screenwriter once, thinking myself quite brilliant for having figured this out all by myself, only to be told by him: "Oh yeah! 'Sex at Sixty'!" That was the term he and his screenwriting buddies used for the "kiss at the first hour." It just goes to show that where the basics of storytelling are concerned, nothing changes.

As suggested, most movies have two intertwining skeins:

The A Story is the hero's tangible goal, what he wants.

The B Story is the hero's spiritual goal, what he needs.

The A Story is what is happening on the surface. It's the plot. The B Story, or what I call the "helper story," helps push the hero to learn the spiritual lesson that every story is really all about. Most often the B Story is "the love interest" aka "the girl." The hero enters the upside-down version of the world of Act Two, looks across a crowded room, and there she is — the person who'll help him on his way to transformation, and hold his hand as he dies and is reborn! And, of course, because she can't be with him when they meet (otherwise where'd we have to go?), the process of boy wins girl, boy loses girl, boy gets girl back in a poker game, is seen time and again in a thousand forms.

"The girl" can also be "the mentor." Check out the B Story of the hit comedy *Dodgeball: A True Underdog Story*. Who's the B Story? Who's the "helper" character that will push hero Vince Vaughn to learn his lesson in leadership? Why it's Rip Torn, as down-and-out ex-dodgeball champ, Patches O'Houlihan! Proof comes when seeing how the B Story beats of that movie line up. We first meet Patches on page 30, when Vince and his team see an old dodgeball instructional film starring the younger Patches (Hank Azaria). At Midpoint, the stakes are raised, and A and B cross, when an older Patches arrives in the flesh and — publicly — tells Vince that he is now the team's coach. Since all mentors go to page 75 to die, Patches does too, giving Vince pause before pushing him to action in Act Three, where Patches even reappears — *en spirito* — to give Vince the ghostly final shove he needs to go on to dodgeball greatness. Rudimentary? Yes. Silly? Of course!

And yet this basic construct appears again and again.

Whether the B Story is one person like a love interest, mentor, or sidekick, or a group such as the host of helpers the heroes learn from in the Act Two worlds of *Legally Blonde*, *Miss Congeniality*, and *Gladiator*, these B Story pulse points denote the function of forcing the hero to learn his real lesson.

And all of it ties back into Theme!

Keep in mind the only reason for storytelling and why A and B must cross throughout: It's to show the true reason for the journey is not getting the tangible goal, but learning the spiritual lesson that can only be found through the B Story!

The Theme Stated moment on page 5 of a well-structured screenplay ties in to the lesson the hero will learn. This is the place, up front, when you as writer get to say what this movie is about — and it might take a few drafts to enunciate precisely. A clue for finding it is seeing how the B Story "helps" the hero learn the lesson. When you do figure it out, state the lesson up front, tie it to the B Story's introduction on page 30, the raising of the stakes at Midpoint, the **moment of clarity** that helps the hero realize his error in Dark Night of the Soul, and the final push into Act Three the hero needs to learn his lesson — and triumph.

OTHER INTERESTING PHENOMENA

The various sections of the Transformation Machine are each different. They serve a different need, have a different tone, and yet all point to the same goal: *change*. They also help troubleshoot our brilliant ideas that don't quite fit, or that we don't quite know what to do with — and even help with the problem of selling our scripts. The Fun and Games is a great example of this.

"Fun and Games" is my term, and indicates, I hope, where the "promise of the premise" of a movie is found. It's the part where the hero first enters and explores the Antithesis world — and it's "fun" to the extent that we are not as concerned with plot as we are with seeing what this new world is about. But this term has also led to confusion. What's "fun" about the series of bodies found in this section of many murder mysteries and slasher flicks? What's "fun" about Russell Crowe in *Gladiator* being given up for dead and learning the ropes of *Spartacus*-like combat? While not every Fun and Games section is purely fun, it does offer us a cool way to troubleshoot the problem of figuring out what the poster of your movie is, if you don't know. Why?

Because the Fun and Games is your pitch!

I can't tell you the a-ha! moment that occurred for me when this fact hit me. I was trying to help a writer get her adventure go-ing. *It's like* Miss Congeniality, *I was telling her, by the time you hit page 25, the story is on! Tomboy FBI agent, Sandra Bullock, is undercover...* Then a lightbulb. I saw Sandra in her gown, crown, and sash, a gun in her garter. That's the Fun and Games of *Miss Congeniality*.

It's the poster!

It's the concept!

To me, a guy very concerned with delivering on his premise, I thought that was enough to worry about. But knowing this new twist, I can also reverse engineer both what goes into Fun and Games and how to double-check to make sure it's my movie's crux.

This is an important a-ha! because when you're trying to figure out what your story is, you will pitch all kinds of things: Setting, Theme, Catalyst, even the Finale of your tale.

I've heard them all. And they're all *not* your movie.

No, the movie is not where it's set. It's not its "meaning." It's not how the hero is "called to action." And it's not the big slam-bang Finale — even though all these are vital.

It's the Fun and Games. That's your movie.

And if your Fun and Games section isn't solid, or isn't deliv-ering on your premise, now's the time to find out.

Looking at the map on page 47, and seeing all the pieces of this flow chart, helps us see other points of interest, too, ones which, while I stood at the whiteboard, led to similar a-ha! moments.

One really interesting point of comparison is the similarity between two sections: *"Catalyst — Debate — Break into Two"* and *"All Is Lost — Dark Night of the Soul — Break into 3."*

Just look at how these sets of plot points line up:

— *Catalyst* and *All Is Lost* are both points where something is done to the hero. In Catalyst, it's innocent, an invitation, a telephone call, the discovery of news that starts the adventure. The All Is Lost is also done to the hero, but it's more serious: This is where he's evicted, fired, loses his significant other, or someone dies. It's a different tone, but the same function.

— *Debate* and *Dark Night of the Soul* also are alike. It's... hesitation. Having received an invitation or, later, when the stakes are more serious, and having experienced a death, jail, or exile... now what? Again, the difference is that early on the consequences are few; later, more serious. But the function is the same: Given a life-altering jolt, what will the hero do next?

— *Break into Two* and *Break into Three* is the response. Both are proactive moves on the part of the hero that take him to the next level. Having been hit with something, and thought about it, the hero now acts. Here again, the stakes are more serious later on because we are just about to face "the final test."

And all these sections of your movie are designed to do what the entire Transformation Machine is set up to accomplish: Force change in the hero or heroes — and in us, the audience.

So are we done yet? Not quite.

THE FIVE-POINT FINALE

When it comes to "structure dilemmas," no part of a story can be more frustrating than Act Three — one about which I realize I am guilty of not revealing all. I have been amused by how often I get called out on point #14 in my 15-point Blake Snyder Beat Sheet — the one that is simply labeled "Finale." "Well, thanks a pantload, Blake," is the gist of the objection. And while I say the basis of this section is Synthesis, it doesn't seem quite enough. Where is the little red button that Tommy Lee Jones told Will Smith not to touch in *Men in Black* that *Save the Cat!* is known for? Because when you're deep in it, and have tried every trick you can to solve the problem, I want you to not only have that button, but to push it!

I am most excited about what I call the "Five-Point Finale" because by using it you can finish *any* story. And though I've had a version in my back pocket for a while, it wasn't until I began helping writers that I realized how useful it is. We've seen how the hero is thrown into the Transformation Machine and forced to change, but how do you finish this process? Synthesis gives us one clue. But when it comes to figuring out what to *do*, I hope you will soon be rocketing upside down through the Holland Tunnel smiling — and thinking fondly of me.

In addition to Act Three being about Synthesis, the Third Act Finale is best seen as the "Final Exam" for the hero. Having started off naively, and been schooled in the world of hard knocks, he has died and been given the chance to be born anew. But has he learned his lesson? And can he apply it? There is no better way to show this test than in what I call **Storming the Castle**, the essence of every ending and the key to the Five-Point Finale.

What is the "castle"? And what are these five points?

1. *Gathering the Team* — The first step, once the hero has decided to proactively cross into Act Three, is the "Gathering of the Team," those he'll need to "storm the castle." The **castle** can be anything, from an actual fortress (the "Death Star" in *Star Wars*), to getting on stage at a local rock club (*School of Rock*), to helping your girl reach the airport (*Casablanca*), to "rushing to the airport" to stop your girl from leaving without you (*Love Actually*). A big part of being able to do this is the rallying of allies, who may not be on speaking terms with the hero at the moment, and "amending hurts" to be able to work together. It also involves "gathering tools," and making plans for what we hope will be a successful run at the task at hand. This includes "strapping on the guns" in *The Matrix*, when Keanu Reeves and Carrie-Anne Moss literally choose the weapons they'll need to storm the castle and free their captured mentor Morpheus (Laurence Fishburne) from the clutches of... those guys.

2. *Executing the Plan* — The second step is the actual "Storming of the Castle" when the execution of the plan feels foolproof. Sure it's a challenge, and there must be some sense in every Storming of the Castle that "this is crazy." In fact, that very line is heard in many Finales just to let you in the audience know what an impossible task is at hand. "This can't be done" is key to setting up the challenge our heroes face. But as the plan begins to unfold, by gum, we just might pull off this crazy plan! We're succeeding! The team is working together like a well-oiled machine. In many instances this is also where we pay off the arcs and proofs of growth for the minor characters, and show how that defect they had at the beginning of the story is now "fixed" — and even useful — thanks to the journey the hero dragged his pals along on. It's all looking good here. And yet there is a sense as the goal nears that this is too easy. Sure we've lost some nameless soldiers, who demonstrate their loyalty by taking a bullet for the team (Randy Quaid in *Independence Day*, Rhys Ifans in *Notting Hill*, those way-too-happy-to-die pilots in *Star Wars*), but the crew is together and the High Tower in sight.

3. *The High Tower Surprise* — The third step in the Five-Point Finale proves how overly optimistic that assessment was. For this is the part where the hero reaches the High Tower where the princess is being kept and finds something shocking: no princess! (For a twist on the "Princess," check out the Five-Point Finale of *Enchanted*, which proves Princesses can often save their own damn selves, thank you very much!) But the point is made: The High Tower Surprise shows we were not only overly confident in our plan — overconfidence is one of the problems! Seems not only is the plan dashed, but the Bad Guy, or the forces aligned against our hero, "knew we were coming" all along. This is the part where "traitors are exposed" and our brilliant plan is revealed to be a trap set by the Bad Guys (as Russell Crowe in *Gladiator* discovers when his plot to rally Rome and overthrow Joaquin Phoenix proves to be doomed from the start). The effort now comes to a dead stop. The hero and his allies are

"arrested in their tracks," and the "clock is ticking" on our doom. It looks like all is lost *again!* However smart our hero thought he was up to this point, however much he's done to "synthesize" his lesson by reuniting his allies and giving it his all... it's not enough. The shock of the High Tower Surprise is learning that's not what this effort has been about. And the real challenge of the Final Exam the hero must pass is about to become clear.

4. "*Dig, Deep Down*" — The whole point of the Finale now is revealed — and it's not what we expected. This is the part where all human solution is exhausted. This is where we've got *bupkis*; there's not a back-up plan, nor an alternate course in sight. And it's all come down to the hero — who's got nothing either. Yet, as it turns out... *this* is the true test! In a sense, every story is about the "stripping away" of the stuff the hero thinks is important at the start of the story, including his own little ideas for winning at the end. This is the part where the hero has to find that last ounce of strength to win but can't use normal means to do so. And lest you think this is a goofy, "formula" thing, in fact it is the whole point of storytelling. For this is the part we've waited for, the "touched-by-the-divine" beat where the hero lets go of his old logic and does something he would never do when this movie began.

Devoid of a human solution, the hero returns to the blackness he succumbed to during the cocoon stage of his transformation to prove he's mastered that part of himself that is beyond human to find faith, inner strength, a last-ditch idea, love, grace. It's the Dig-Deep-Down moment all stories teach us: At some point we have to abandon the natural world, and everything we think we know, and have faith in a world unseen. This is the part in *Star Wars* where we hear Obi-Wan say: "Use the Force, Luke!"; the part of *Gladiator* when, seemingly dead, Russell Crowe finds that last bit of energy to stab Joaquin Phoenix right in his Coliseum. It's the part where Hugh Grant dares speak to Julia Roberts in the press conference finale of *Notting Hill*, and in *Indiana Jones and the Last Crusade* when

Harrison Ford is given a choice to save his father (Sean Connery) by giving up everything else. It's the part in *Planes, Trains and Automobiles* where Steve Martin, having figured out John Candy has no wife, recalls the lonely man that has become his friend and goes back to rescue him. This is the moment of faith when, with a breathless gasp, the trapeze artist, high up in the darkness of the big top, lets go of his grip on the world, does his spin, and snaps out into the void hoping another will take his hands. And we watch in anticipation, for in our own way... we've been waiting, too.

5. *The Execution of the New Plan* — The answer comes from a place we've all hoped is real, but only the hero has faith enough to trust, and when he does, he wins... and so do we. Awakened to the true lesson of this story, the hero puts this last-ditch plan into action and it works! This is where "on the fly" the hero tries it a new way — and succeeds. Thinking fast, Humphrey Bogart's plan prevails in *Casablanca*; risking all, Dustin Hoffman grabs Katharine Ross and runs in *The Graduate*; going with his gut, Dev Patel answers the final question that will make him a *Slumdog Millionaire*. It was only by stepping into the unknown — and trusting — that the hero could find the way to triumph. *This* is the test. Can you give up belief in your old ways and have faith in the dark, quiet place inside? Rewards go to those who seek this moment in fiction and in life. It's the reason we tell stories and honor those who understand. This is why, when we go to the Final Image of a movie — such as the ceremony at the end of *Star Wars* — we feel like we won as well.

Because we did!

Believe it or not, this Five-Point Storming the Castle occurs in some form or fashion in *every* story! This is the "face-your-fear" part, the final test that proves the hero was paying attention — or not! And yet the risk of putting this out there is to once again hear cries of "formula!" To which I say, *phooey!*

The Five-Point Finale is your secret weapon for finding the true meaning of your tale. And that Dig-Deep-Down point, that

"Use the Force, Luke!" beat, is what we're all looking for whether we are the writers of the story or the audience for it. Yes, this way of looking at the ending of any story also works when the hero or heroes are "Defending the Castle" as seen in the finales of *Saving Private Ryan*, *Shaun of the Dead*, and *Blazing Saddles* — or in "Escaping the Castle" as seen in *Alien*, *Free Willy*, and *Defiance*. Whether your team is on the offense or the defense, the lessons of friendship, teamwork, selflessness, and nobility are the same, and the Dig-Deep-Down moment is key. No matter what the permutation of your tale, it's the dynamic we seek, for the need of any story boils down to being touched by powers unseen.

Special effects are fine, great set pieces are wonderful, funny jokes and unique characters are vital. But if you take me to the divine in your story, I will tell all my friends about it.

That's what storytelling is really about.

And that kind of magic is as far from formula as it gets.

LET'S REVIEW

My goal is much simpler, however: to help you avoid feeling stuck. Between the ease of the BS2, the visual clarity of The Board, and this latest structure map, you should feel fully empowered. You now have the Wurlitzer keyboard at your command. You can set the tempo, rhythm, and structure for every story! Using these tools, you can finesse your way through any structure snag. And though we'll get into all new monkey wrenches in the next chapters as we deal with actual notes from executives and others, for now you can feel good. You have all kinds of new ways to throw your curveballs, spitballs, sliders, and fastballs.

But perhaps you're still feeling penned in?

If you can't shake the feeling that structure isn't helping you feel "free," I understand. It's a common hesitation. Using the BS2 and working out the 15 beats, then going to The Board, you may still think it's all too easy, too mechanical, too formulaic. You are "All Beat Out... with Nowhere to Go" — dressed to the nines, picture perfect, but unmotivated to continue on to the show. Well, if that's the case, you have to shake it up. You have to get out of the structure and tell the story in a new way. I have used these tactics to do so:

▸ *My movie: the one page* — This is the trick famed screenwriter William Goldman uses. He will not start writing his screenplay until he can tell his story in one page; he gives himself 300 words and no more to tell the tale. This forces him to get to the crux of his story.

▸ *My movie: the tone poem* — I'm not kidding. I have often retold my story as a poem. In rhyming couplets, with all brand new challenges to get across what my story is, sometimes I have had all new breakthroughs, and sometimes all new story ideas!

▸ *My movie: the comedy* — Perhaps you're too wrapped up in tone? Is your story overly dramatic, overly comic? Try pitching the opposite. If a drama, try the comedic take to shake it up.

▸ *My movie: the Rubik's Cube* — One of the nice aspects of the *STC!* software is the ability to move scenes around at will. Try it. Take them off the board, shuffle, and randomly put them back up out of order. You never know what insights will be realized.

Anything you can do to free your story, frees you too. It lets you deal with the continuing elasticity of your tale. All the way through, from the first *Save the Cat!* to this chapter, I hope I've stressed the nimbleness required, the talent to — at any minute — throw away everything you hold near and dear, and try something brand new. And nowhere is this particular challenge greater than when we have actually executed a script and are now staring at the result. Panic. Self-Recrimination. Grief. These are just some of the emotional candy we snack on when we know something's wrong — and we don't know how to solve it.

But fear not.

The Script Doctor is in!

chapter 4

Blake's Blog /
June 23, 2008

"Story is a puzzle.
And getting all
the pieces to fit
just right... is the
point of the job."

STRAIGHTENING YOUR SPINE

As much as I enjoy teaching classes and responding to your email, one of the most delightful experiences I've had since writing *Save the Cat!* is working with you one-on-one. Though I have written or co-written 78 scripts, there is nothing I like more than reading and reviewing your screenplay — primarily due to one simple fact:

It's not my script!

Yes, just like in class, as I so pleasantly rip your Fun and Games to shreds, or bluntly say "No, that doesn't work," or smile while you are seemingly lost, it's so much easier to see a problem when I'm not emotionally involved. But whether it's me, or the writers in your writing group, or your agent, or a civilian with no vested interest, someone has to read your screenplay. Bringing your idea to its final form is perilous, but a must.

It's like *The Wages of Fear*. Ever see this? French film. Two truck drivers have to deliver a load of nitroglycerin — very slowly — through an obstacle course of rope bridges and quicksand. And they're French, so there's all that Gauloises smoke.

Well that's us, minus the Turkish cigarettes hopefully, assigned to transport this wonderful little flicker of inspiration across the finish line by extrapolating just the right story from it. Yet the highway is riddled with warnings of what happens when we fail to heed the laws of sound storytelling.

One of the movies I mentioned earlier as a great example of a title that grabs us is *Snakes on a Plane*. Yes, great title, great concept! But I bet even those connected with the film feel they never quite delivered on the promise of the premise.

Booooooom!

It just shows what can happen.

A great title and logline are vital, for without attracting attention to our story with a concept that grabs us, we will not get the chance we deserve to have our screenplay bought and made. But we still have to *ex-e-cute*. And that means nailing down the *sto-ry*.

And that means checking out something called "the spine."

SCRATCHING YOUR SPINE

What is the so-called **spine of the story**?

That's simple. The spine is how we track what happens to the hero or heroes from the beginning to the end. It's that thing we follow, the rail we keep tabs on with our toe in the dark, as we watch a hero we love, or at least understand, grow and change.

And that change must be big!

Heroes start off one way and end up another. In the comedy *Liar Liar*, Jim Carrey is a liar when we start that movie and by the end he's not. What happened? The spine of the story shows Jim's "milestones of growth" as he goes from one polar extreme to its opposite. And the bigger the change for any hero, the better.

The problem for us is that anything that doesn't add to the spine, doesn't belong. And that's when the trouble starts.

Great stories come about only with a lot of banging away on the story spine to make sure it's straight — and stays straight — because the temptation to veer off the path is tremendous. We're writers! We are lured away by flashes of light in the bushes that take us off the road and into the brambles. And the harder we try to incorporate these misadventures — the more we justify mistakes and convince ourselves inspiration trumps all — the faster we find ourselves with **story scoliosis**, a crooked spine of a tale chock full of half-steps, missteps, off-ramps, U-turns, and curlicues.

And that's when you come to me.

I love working with writers, and I love pounding on your spine to make sure it's straight. I have objectivity. So when I say your whole Act One has gotta go because it doesn't set up what the hero learns by the end, you think: "What are you, *insane!*? You mean that part I slaved over for two months, and even got the punctuation marks in the right places?"

That's right. Gone-o.

Or when I tell you your Opening Image is wrong, you are dumbfounded. That's the initial scene you think is *sooooooooooo* brilliant because it matches up with the Final Image perfectly. So you say: "That's stupid, *you're* stupid. You don't get it!"

And I have to tell you something that may sound odd:

You're better than this!

You're clinging to stuff not because it's brilliant but because you think, secretly, you can't come up with something else. Deep down you protect these scenes and images because you think they're your best work, and you can't do it any better.

Well, I'm saying you can.

You can come up with a hundred better Opening Images.

You can write a brand spanking new Act One.

In your sleep.

As long as you stick to the one job that is the one thing anyone really cares about: telling a story with a spine.

And cutting out anything that doesn't service that mission.

WHO'S THE HERO?

One of the first things to figure out in any story, and one of the fastest ways to get taken off the rails if we don't, is to discover *whom* this is about. When you give me your script and I have a problem with it, this is the first question I usually ask:

Who's the hero?

Because what I'm really asking is: Are you sure?

In class, I talk about this as it relates to my script, *Granny*. Ask anyone; this is a screenplay I'd been working on for years. I had 10 drafts of *Granny* that did not sell. And one of the reasons it didn't was... I had the wrong hero.

Granny, you'll recall, is the story of a senior serial killer who arrives on a family's doorstep claiming to be the recently dead wife's mother, and here's the scene: It's a dark and stormy night. (Sorry) There's a knock at the door. Standing there is a sweet old lady (and recent escapee from St. Vitus Center for the Criminally Insane). Who answers the door? Dad. Because in the early drafts, Dad was the hero. The story was about the head of the house, wife dead, children out of control, who needs lots of help.

So when Granny shows up, he says *come on in!*

Well, for target market reasons, that was really a bad idea. Men over 40 don't see these slasher flicks; teenagers do!

So how does the scene play now?

Same dark and stormy night. Same stranger on the stoop.

But now it's Amber, the 16-year-old, who answers the door.

Now it's her story. And that's the draft that sold.

You may have different problems finding your hero that aren't related to figuring out the target market. Sometimes, there are two people we need to track, so whom are we tracking most? Take *Lethal Weapon*. Like most buddy movies, this is what we call a "two-hander" because both Danny Glover and Mel Gibson change. But the way to find the spine is to see it as Danny's story; he's the one with the case, and the problem — and he's the one who'll be most affected by his time spent with suicidal Mel.

There are also films with three heroes. Examples of expertise in dealing with these can be found in the work of Ted Elliott and Terry Rossio, who apparently like this dynamic. Check out *Aladdin*, then compare and contrast with the first *Pirates of the Caribbean* and realize these are both brilliant examples of a "three-hander." But Terry will tell you while *Aladdin* is the title character's movie, *Pirates* is really Keira Knightley's story; that's how they charted the spine. By zeroing in on one hero, and tracking events through her, these two screenwriting greats got a handle on "Who's the hero?" — and as a result found their spine.

But the fun doesn't end there.

If yours is an ensemble piece, like *Crash* or *Babel*, who's the hero then? Well in those cases, it's several people with several story arcs. But we still have to find the spine — and that is found in the *issue* of each movie. *Crash* is about isolation. *Babel* is about global interconnectedness. And each has an "entry-point character" (Don Cheadle in *Crash*, Brad Pitt in *Babel*) who's "us" and who, slightly above the fray, has his eyes opened the most.

If you're having a hard time finding your hero, try this handy guide to figuring out who it is, and whose story you must follow as he goes from beginning to end. The hero is the one who:

- is most like "us"
- has the biggest "arc"
- learns the greatest lesson
- least wants to change, yet...
- has the most need to do so

And the only reason to figure this out is so we can keep our story spine straight. Knowing the "who" tells us how to demarcate the "milestones of growth" and the change the hero makes from beginning to end.

So how do we show that change?

WHAT'S THE PROBLEM?

How you show the change is by asking, *What's the problem?* This is the second question I pose to struggling writers about their scripts, after we've established whom their movie concerns. A hero has to have a problem that this movie will fix, so if your movie doesn't start out with a hero and a world with problems, I see it. But you don't. *Yet!* So I am usually smiling — evilly — when I ask:

Why is having no problem a problem?

The short answer is: If there's no problem, you have nowhere to go. If there's nothing wrong, why take this trip?

Keep in mind my most brilliant piece of advice to writers and the thing that brings us all back to square one — and back down to earth: Any story you tell is about "the most important event that ever happened to the hero of that story." It is the most life-altering, most paradigm-shifting, most enlightening or crucial episode — and *this* story causes that change to occur. The problems we set these heroes up with, and resolve in the course of the tale, trump all. Forget all the car crashes, and the set pieces, and the Fun and Games that have drawn us to see this movie; they are only in the service of transforming the hero.

And us.

If you don't see this as your spine; if, at base, you aren't tracking this change, and showing how the change occurs from scene to scene, you will not have a story that matters.

There, I said it!

And let me tell you, it feels good to get it off my chest!

If this declaration is true, and you have every reason to believe it is, then figuring out "the problem" is how you will track "the transformation." If someone is going from Point A to Point B, then you must start your hero off with a problem that's so big and so all-encompassing, it makes the trip worthwhile.

And if not, you have to make it so.

You'll note in the first chapter, when dealing with the logline for *Quickie* — about the banker who goes to Las Vegas and wakes up with a penniless waitress (yay Vegas!) — when breaking down that story we must be able to see more than its poster, we have to see what the movie's "about." And guess what? It's not about the hero's bender, or his job, or his boss; it's the fact he's about to marry the wrong girl. The way to make that point clearer is to show us up front that our hero's soon-to-be future-altering choice will lead to a dead end in all aspects of his life. Yet while even that is true, it's *still* not the problem.

The problem is: Our hero doesn't know it!

And the story spine will track how our hero figures it out.

Stories are about problem solving, and the slow coming to consciousness by our hero that he a) has a deficit and b) needs to fix it. If you don't have a hero with a problem, find one — and make it clear. The bigger the problem, the stronger the spine.

In the three loglines pitched in that first chapter, we can see who the hero is in each, but "what's the problem?" One way to solve broken concepts like these is to ask this question, and be ready to change the concept entirely when we find the answer.

▶ In *Quickie*, the problem is our hero's marriage will lead to a dead-end life; thus, the spine should track how he discovers this and gives up his old ways to embrace the new. And now maybe it's better to describe the waitress he marries as "vivacious" rather than "penniless." That simple adjective switch suddenly makes me see where this might go.

▶ In *Partly Cloudy*, according to the logline, the problem is our TV weatherman is bored, but really it's a story about a coward: A passive man wants to be a hero. That's the "problem" we'll track. So now maybe he should be "on the verge of" hurricane season, and we need to "set up" the idea that saving his town is part of the Act Three finale.

▶ In *Dark Streets*, the problem is he's a down-and-out cop, full of existential angst about his job — and his life, who will learn life's real meaning as he actively solves the mystery. And if the writer can give up "hiding the ball" and tell us this, the real drama might come out!

But it all comes back to finding "the problem."

Having established a problem, anything that is NOT will have to be carefully weighed in each of these concepts. If a story point doesn't directly relate to the spine, out it goes!

And if you can't find the problem, try harder! In truth we, the audience, don't care what you pick. The hero's deficit doesn't matter as long as you set it up and show the problem evolve through the movie. This is why I'm so cavalier when I read your script. I know that as an audience what I'm really looking for is not your brilliant imagery, but a character with a problem, who changes. Together we'll find it; we just have to look.

I have a wonderful little motto that I use with writers: **Force it**. You can apply this to any screenwriting dilemma, for it forces you to make changes you may not think you need. If you don't feel like figuring it out, or have no idea, make it up! This is the joy of "forcing it" — and it works.

I also have another great troubleshooting slogan I'll introduce at this point. It's something I like to call **Here's the bad way to do this**. Like the beautiful simplicity of "force it," this lets us recalcitrant writers off the hook. Can't come up with a problem for the hero of your movie? Say: "Here's the bad way to do this" and proceed to tell us something dumb.

It takes the pressure off.

And it very often is not only *not* dumb, it's the solution.

SNIPPING THE ENDS

How does the hero begin this movie and how does he end up? This is the third question I always pose when dealing with story scoliosis, especially when I am not seeing the hero change. I've suggested you know who the hero is, and also tell us his problem. And make sure that problem is huge! But I need to know more.

Most stories are about an underdog, and establishing the world he lives in is part of explaining why he's the way he is. The hero is an underdog because he has defects of character that cause him to be so, fear mostly — and any number of behaviors masquerading as fear. But his "world" is also deficient. It's a world where they pray to the sun every day, and when the sun rises, all hail the king who organized this ritual. Only we the audience, and our hero, suspect the king is a sham. By story's end, the hero's life must be turned upside-down. It's not enough for him to win; he must expose the king — and transform the kingdom! — to truly succeed.

Stacking the deck against the hero at the start of your story is part of what I call "snipping the ends." How does your hero start this tale, and how does he end it? That start and finish had better be extremes. We set up his home life, work life, and play life; these are all part of his world. But by the end, these aspects must be wholly new. When figuring out where the story begins and where it ends, change is your guide.

To show what I mean, and to let those who believe I'm only talking about "formula" movies — that you think Hollywood squeezes out like so much Play-Doh — let's look at three Academy Award®-nominated screenplays for 2007. Each of these screenplays has picture-perfect opening and closing images that are the right ones because the writer has properly snipped the ends of the story:

▶ *The Savages* — Laura Linney begins this movie repressed sexually and professionally, and belittled by dominating brother, Philip Seymour Hoffman. By the end she's a successful playwright and has dumped her bald, overbearing lover in favor of... his dog.

▶ *Michael Clayton* — George Clooney is on the run from his law firm, uncertain of his life or character, and broke. By the end he's left the firm, turned the tables on them, and is parleying a million-dollar settlement with "Company Man" Tilda Swinton.

▶ *Lars and the Real Girl* — Ryan Gosling starts bereft, due to his mother's death, and alone. By the end, he's made peace with his mom at her gravesite — and found the "real girl" who loves him.

In each of these stories we ask: "What happened?" What caused this remarkable, life-altering change? It begins with picking the Alpha-Omega, the snapshot of the world before this movie began... and after. If you don't have that, or can't answer the question yet, or aren't *forcing* these changes to occur in your story...

Do.

THE TANGIBLE AND THE SPIRITUAL

Just to pile it on while I've got your attention, let's talk about goals: yours and your hero's. *What is your hero's goal?* is the fourth question I ask writers. And again, when I do, it's because it's missing from your story — or not apparent.

Every hero in every good story has to demonstrate a burning desire to do something and be proactive about it throughout. In addition, that hero has a lesson to learn, a change to experience that is the subterranean story, and in truth the real reason for the tale. In most writing classes, you'll hear this described as the "wants and needs" of the hero. A baseball star *wants* to win the big game; what he *needs* is a lesson in teamwork. But to me, it's more than that, and these two types of goals touch on a more important aspect of storytelling: the reason we do this job!

I prefer to think of "wants and needs" as **the tangible and the spiritual**. Both the "tangible" (wants) and the "spiritual" (needs) are important and must be shown in your hero's story — and I want to know both, even with the very briefest of pitches. That's because these two very distinct goals work together and have to be tracked throughout. One without the other is an empty experience, and so we must knit hard to weave them together.

"What is the hero's actual goal?" "What concrete thing is he after?" is usually what I ask when the tangible isn't clear. I cite the Little League trophy Walther Matthau chases in *The Bad News Bears* (1976), the job promotion Mel Gibson seeks in *What Women Want*, the missing soldier Tom Hanks searches for in *Saving Private Ryan*.

And btw, the hero has to pursue these things with vigor.

The goal has to be tangible because if you tell me that your hero wants "peace on earth" or "to make the world a better place," I will ask you: When does he know he can stop? To be a "tangible" goal, it has to be something you can actually quantify, a thing, something we can know for sure when he's won or lost. If that isn't the case, you are blurring the goals.

Because the point of the story involves more.

The "spiritual" goal is why we're really going on this trip. Just like in life, you may want all kinds of things — a better job, a bigger house, the right mate, admittance to the cool clubs — but what we're looking for is much deeper. What we seek is a spiritual connection, the sense of something important happening in our lives, the proof that whether we get what we want or not, there is a point to being here. And whether yours is a silly comedy, big action piece, slasher flick, or musical, the invisible underpinning of why we go along on your trip must be known by you and constantly reinforced throughout your story.

It's all about showing a hero with twin goals — seen and unseen, concrete and invisible, actively sought and conferred.

Take *Maria Full of Grace*, a wonderful Indie I dissect in my second book, about a pregnant girl in a small South American town who takes on a dangerous mission by becoming a drug mule. Like the hero of the movie I cite at the start of this chapter, *The Wages of Fear*, Maria is stuck in a South American town, facing a lifeless future. Both movies begin their protagonist's journey all the way back behind the eight ball of life. In both cases, the tangible goal of each character is palpable: to earn the money to get out! It's why each decides to risk his or her life.

Yet beneath the tangible goal that drives the plot is a spiritual one that's the real story. In *Maria Full of Grace*, to change her world, Maria thinks she has to leave it. In fact, she just has to see the world in a different way. By movie's end, the money she risked all to earn has been lost; she's adrift in America, homeless, friendless, back to square one. The difference is: She's proud. And happy! The tangible goal she thought she really wanted has been replaced by something divine. Love, hope, friendship, gratitude, new ways of thinking — and, yes, grace — are divine. And like the problem that is solved in all good stories, in Maria's case... the solution is the last thing she expected!

When I ask about the tangible and spiritual goals of your hero, that's what I mean. On the surface, what actual goal is driving your hero? And below the surface, at the hidden level that is your real story, what does your hero need? And get?

Here is an easy way to remember these two threads that must intertwine within every well-structured tale:

▸ The "tangible" — is the A Story, the concrete goal driving your hero at every given point along the way; it is "the plot."

▸ The "spiritual" — is the B Story, the below-the-surface tale that is the "lesson" your hero will learn and "the theme."

Isn't this stuff about as cool as it gets?

THE ARC OF THE EXPERIENCE

What we are talking about here, keep in mind, is making, and keeping, the spine of your story straight throughout.

And the solution is like clear mountain spring water.

Once we see it.

We need a hero who starts *waaaay* back at the beginning, and is pocked with problems. He is at a loss, in fear, pushed down, held back, and may not even know it! His is a world, in fact, that in every part of his life — at work, at home, and at play — looks at him like he's from Mars. And in his own way, he is. His is a backstory with all manner of Achilles heels, assorted recurring nightmares he can't quite shake, defects of character that stop him from enjoying life to its fullest — and whether he is Donald Trump rolling in the dough-ray-me, or a homeless bum on the skids, he reminds us of someone we know very well: ourselves.

And, like him, we know *somethin's* gotta give... and soon.

Once he is sent off on his mission (this very cool little pitch you've come up with), we have armed him with such a tangible goal, and such a driving desire to get to the end, he can't help but keep moving — and we can't help but hope he makes it. He's the detective on the case, the soldier on the march, the girl who burns to find true love. And by the end, when they reach their last beat, they have been so awakened to the real meaning of the trip, they dare to do something so breathtakingly new, that the world they left, or came back to, will be changed forever, as in upside-down.

And we say: *mama!*

What a ride.

That's all we're looking for. That's how to straighten your spine! And don't be confused by the hundreds of movies you see that don't have this, that get away with murder at the Cineplex.

I know I can't be the only one who's noticed!

I'm the guy who sits in lots of movies and when my date and I leave, I say: "Nothing happened." "What are you talking about?" she says. "Didn't you see all those special effects, those car chases, those hilarious jokes?" Yes, I did. What I didn't catch was a story. What I missed was a hero with a problem who in the course of this movie extravaganza learns something and changes.

And so it is not surprising that the movie we all rushed to see in the first week — due to the great special effects and the funny trailer moments and all the other "stuff" — drops off the radar in the second week. Box office falls 50 or 60 or even 70% and everyone wonders why. It's because what the movie gave audiences was only so much fluff. There was lots of stuff happening, when actually nothing happened at all. And all the movie had to give me was just a tiny bit of a story, something I can use in my life here on Earth. They need to show me a guy with a problem who changes and grows for the journey.

I need that.

And so do you.

Which leads me to the fifth and final question I ask a strug-gling, spine-scoliosied writer who (picture Igor: *Yeth, Math-ter!*) comes to me wondering why his screenplay is crooked:

What's it about?

The good news is: By answering this question, you will know everything about your movie. It's the theme of your film, and we know how important theme is.

The bad news is: You may not know what it is until the end!

Here's a story...

As part of my duties in *Cat!*dom, I gave a speech to the talented writers and artists at a major studio's animation division. It was maybe the highlight of my career. Having been a writer with an office on that lot, to return "home" was one of the great moments of my life. Later, I listened while a group of 40 animators went over a project they were working on, and were, by their own admission, stuck. The session was designed to un-stick them.

The problem was, they not only didn't know what the ending was, they couldn't settle on the Midpoint, or how it segued into Act Three. Versed in *Save the Cat!* (many of the animators have both *Cats!* by their work stands — *Yes!*), we batted around "All Is Lost" and the "Dark Night of the Soul" but couldn't get a handle on any of it, until I asked what seemed an obvious question:

What's it about?

At which point everyone jumped in *en masse* and said they had five different takes, and five different ways to go, and we all real-ized that's why they had no ending — they had no theme! Without knowing why they were telling the story, they could not find what it meant to have one ending or another, one lesson or another, one direction or another. Without knowing "What's it about?" they had no compass. And without one, they were lost.

I bring this up to let you know even steely pros with years of experience, scads of talent, and working at major studios, fall into the same traps as you and I. I also know that the answer isn't always clear. Many times it's only after I or my partners have written THE END and dropped the script in the outgoing mail that we suddenly say: *Wait! I know what it's about! And I know where to stick in the line that lets the audience know what that is!*

But sometimes it's only with objectivity that we see it.

We were dancing around it the whole time!

What's the guide for finding the theme in your movie? Well, here's another great fix-it tool I'll put out there: Make a list. No matter what writing problem we're facing, by sitting down with a blank piece of paper, labeling it, as an example, "30 Bad Ideas for the Theme of My Story," and not stopping until you blast out all 30, somewhere among those 30 bad ones will be a great one. It will be THE one. For help on solving Theme, here are some hints:

- ▶ What does the hero learn?
- ▶ What is the moral of the story?
- ▶ What's on your mind? What statement, issue, or ax to grind finds voice in your characters?
- ▶ If the theme were your title, what would it be?
- ▶ What film is yours most like and what's its lesson?

And so... if you follow the rules of how to find the spine of your story, paying attention to all five major questions posed, something truly amazing will occur:

You will find the answers faster than you ever have!

CASE STUDIES:
SCRIPT SOLUTIONS USING THE FIVE QUESTIONS

All this is well and good, Blake, but can you give us some examples of how these rules of yours actually work in real scripts and give us more advice on how to fix these?

Why thanks for asking, anonymous voice in my head.

I'd be glad to!

Here are three case studies that show just what I mean:

CASE STUDY #1 – "Brian B.'s Hero Quest" – Writer Brian B. had the problem of deciding *whom* his story was about. His idea was based on a friend of his who met a woman at a convention of therapists who told a remarkable tale of her adventures during World War Two as a French resistance fighter. As interesting as that is, what's the story?

Brian started by assuming the protagonist was the woman. She was the most interesting character; why shouldn't she be the lead? But by being open to: *Who's the hero?* Brian and I realized a better protagonist might be another, a younger man or woman, also a therapist, who comes to the convention facing a dilemma. What about the older woman's story would make a difference to *this* hero?

We next asked: *What's the problem?* and came up with one that made the hero's dilemma match the lesson the woman passed on. Now it's not just a flashback to World War Two, but a "story within a story" about betrayal. The woman's story helps our hero realize he has betrayed another, and his "coming into awareness" that this is his problem is the spine and how we demarcated his "milestones of growth." By the time our hero leaves the convention, he knows what he has to do to make amends for his wrong deeds — all thanks to "the most important event that ever happened to the hero of this story."

CASE STUDY #2 – "Jerry C.'s Hero Is Too Good" – Jerry C. had a great romantic comedy: a mismatched pair of lovers, one a Border Patrol Agent, the other a fiery Mexican illegal, and a hot topic — immigration. *Illegal Love* speaks to these issues, and yet we were having a hard time getting it off the ground. Why? The male half of the romantic duo was a little too good. Good job, good family, nice guy, with the result that when he gets together with his female half — the fireworks weren't an explosion but a fizzle.

Were we "snipping the ends" as much as we could? When I asked Jerry that very question, he admitted that he didn't want to take his hero "all the way back" because he didn't want him to appear unlikable — so he made him already half-evolved. But if that's the case, why does he need this adventure? How are he and his world one way at the beginning and opposite by the end?

I often talk about *Romancing the Stone* when this problem comes up. One of the reasons it works is because protagonist Joan Wilder (Kathleen Turner) is a socially frozen author when the movie starts. She lives alone, has a wild imagination and one friend — her agent. If she were more evolved, or more daring in life, if she dated, or even left her apartment occasionally, it wouldn't be nearly as much fun when she meets Michael Douglas in the jungles of Colombia.

Well, same here. Odd things happen when we don't take the hero "all the way back." It torques everything and makes the story spine crooked. Not only is snipping the ends not big enough, but the Fun and Games of the movie is less fun. Isn't it better for our hero to loudly denounce illegal immigration at the start? And won't it be more fun when the hero is thrown together with the one woman who will change him by being someone who's not only illegal but equally vehement about the laws?

There are two kinds of problems for a hero at the start: individual and systemic. There must be a personal flaw, an Achilles heel, blind spot, what I call **the shard of glass** buried inside, that this adventure will pull out and force him to deal with — and there must be something wrong with the world, too. Both will get fixed in the course of this story. But to make it work, you have to let go of the notion that your hero is you, take him all the way back to before he becomes evolved, and snip the ends of the story to make sure that your spine is straight!

CASE STUDY #3 — "What's Kathy H.'s Story About?" — One of the best scripts I've consulted on is *Amends* by Kathy H. She is a great writer, and this script is one of the best mysteries I've read in a long while. It concerns an alcoholic Angeleno accused of murdering his wife in a blackout. In the course of the adventure, he discovers his part in her death, and within its twists and turns is a mystery that is also a Rites of Passage tale. Bravo!

But there were two problems: Because of the hero's character and condition, he seemed unmotivated. Both his "tangible goal" and his "spiritual goal" were blurred into a nightmare without direction and a Theme that seemed MIA. Part of Kathy's dilemma was based on the premise: As an alcoholic in the final stages of his disease, the hero didn't care. Even when accused of murder, he ambled from one clue to the next. By giving him a tangible goal — to prove his innocence — we gave the hero a clear driving force.

But where was the spiritual goal? What was this *about*? After hashing it out, we found the Theme... in the title. *Amends* is a story about taking responsibility and making it right, and though the hero finds the truth by script's end, he also realizes his part in his wife's death, which gives this story meaning for both the character and the audience. All because we asked: *What's it about?* and insisted we give the hero both tangible and spiritual goals!

In each of these cases, the story spine was crooked — but how? By asking the five questions, we got to the heart of why, and in each case figured out what was wrong. Storytelling is problem solving, and as long as we approach it as such, without self-recrimination but as steely pros seeking answers, we let go of our fear of being wrong — and just fix it!

And I love the process.

Of course I do. It's not *my* script!

RX FOR STORY SCOLIOSIS

Whether you think you have a crooked spine of a script, or *know* you do, it's best to deal with it by making sure. Story scoliosis, the crooked tale that meanders every which way except the way we want, is no longer a problem... so long as you're aware of your tendency and take note if you wander off the beam.

You must offer us the biggest journey, the greatest change, the most dramatic beginning and end, and meaning in buckets. It must have a hero who changes, and we must be able to show how those

The Wages of Fear: Zut alors, we are stuck in zee mud of our plot. If only I had straightened zee spine of my story!

changes look from the first glimpse of him to the last. We must show milestones of change throughout with breathtaking clarity.

And the easy remedy is this checklist:

The Five Questions to Straighten Your Spine:

1. *Who's the hero?* Whether it's a solo journey like *Maria Full of Grace* or an ensemble like *Crash*, pegging *whom* this story is about is vital; it's who we'll follow from beginning to end.

2. *What's the problem?* Without a set of defects, both in the hero's character and his world, why bother watching? We cavemen are looking for clues to fix our lives, so show us yours!

3. *How does it begin and how does it end?* This is an exercise called Snipping the Ends that you must continually rework. What is the greatest or biggest "- to +" or "+ to -" change for your hero?

4. *What are the tangible and spiritual goals?* The tangible goal is the specific, concrete thing the hero wants; the spiritual goal is the under-story of what the hero needs.

5. *What's it about?* This question relates directly to the spiritual goal. The theme ties in to the B Story, the "helper story" that gives the hero the lesson she really needs to learn.

And if you are having a hard time with any of this, force it. say "Here's the bad way to do this," and if that fails, there's always making a list that will generate the answer!

If you do this, ladies and mens, you can get into that lovely little Citroën truck, light up a Gauloise, and proceed. Whatever package you're carrying — nitroglycerin or Academy Award®-calibre screenplay — you are safe to move on down the highway.

Your spine is straight, your map clearly demarcated, your objective in plain sight. It's blue skies and lollipops for all!

But wait... what's that up ahead??

Blake's Blog /
May 7, 2009

"Words have power.
We know better
than anyone. Let's
make sure our
words are well
chosen."

chapter 5

REWRITE HELL!

"Hell is other people," wrote Jean-Paul Sartre. And for the screenwriter, the experience of dealing with "other people" can certainly *feel* hellish, especially when said people have your script in one hand and an uncapped red Pentel® in the other.

All the wonderful moments you had while writing — the amazing a-ha's, the glorious breakthroughs, the synchronistic chills when everyone seemed to be talking about *your* story — are over. Your script is lying there on a steel table — like the rubbery dude in that *Alien Autopsy* video — while strange men and women with scalpels hover over it, occasionally holding up its gloppy innards, only to inquire in puzzlement: "What the heck is this thing?"

And all you can do is watch.

Your script made sense back in your "writer's room."

But here, in the cold light of Burbank, you're not so sure.

And if you find yourself in a room with executives who have *paid* you for this experience, it's time to not only live with other people, but learn to *love* them — or at least not hate them.

It's time for the "rewrite."

And as important as it is that I and my patrons are all on the same page — literally — this is where the real work starts.

The one thing I became a writer hoping to avoid.

But if we want to continue to be highly paid professionals, or just test our ability to be good and sober citizens, we have to employ all new ways to grin and bear it. So how do we do that — and still maintain the integrity of our story?

Tops on the mind of every writer is the fine line we walk every time we saunter into the studio: Is it our job to speak, on behalf of a script we know better than anyone, by defending every comma? Or are we to just be good sports, go along to get along, and help Og and company realize their vision too — going so far as to incorporate a "vision" we're sure Og came up with by driving past the same billboard we did on our way to the meeting?

If we are to learn one thing from the *Cat!* method, it's that "no man is an island." More than any other creative venture, filmmaking is a group grope, a team sport, and now you must pass the ball, or be passed, or worse, be taken out of the game.

Well, here's a flash: You aren't the only one who's scared.

And I'm here to tell you how wonderful "they" can be and how safe you are in their presence. How do I know? How can I be so assured that your next rewrite will be the best one ever?

Because I will give you 100 years' worth of experience to deal with any crisis in "the room" — and give you a peek into the future of the development process — to let us all... *strike back!*

MY GUYS

I have just returned from a meeting with my writer's group. This small group technique is one I encourage all writers to pursue as they continue to develop their stories. In fact, we have *Cat!* writers groups set up all over the world.

Writers Group: Ben Frahm, Dan Goldberg, Blake Snyder, Dean DeBlois, and Jeremy Garelick on the New York set on the Warner Bros. backlot.

Not to brag or anything, but take a look at who's in mine:

Dan Goldberg, screenwriter of *Meatballs*, *Stripes*, and *Feds*, and now a producer of such hits as *Old School* and *The Hangover*.

Jeremy Garelick, screenwriter of *The Break-Up*, *The Hangover* (uncredited), and the upcoming *Baywatch*.

Dean DeBlois, screenwriter/director of *Lilo & Stitch* and *How to Train Your Dragon*.

And freshman **Ben Frahm**, whose first script, *Dr. Sensitive*, sold to Tom Shadyac and Universal for $350,000 against $500,000.

How did I get so lucky?

Our group got its start thanks to Dan, who in 2007 was giving a talk to screenwriters here in Los Angeles and mentioned *Save the Cat!* as a new favorite. Through the grapevine, I heard this and called up Dan to introduce myself and say thanks! Dan wondered about my *Cat!* workshops and we decided to form a group based on the *Cat!* beats.

Dean had taken my class; so had Ben. In fact it was in one of my early workshops where Ben, new arrival to L.A. via Cornell, worked out the initial beats for *Dr. Sensitive*, and Dean had developed a "Monster in the House" script he sold to Disney. Jeremy and I had met thanks to my manager, Andy Cohen, and was also a *Cat!* fan. We'd often spoken about getting together to pitch ideas and read scripts in progress using *Cat!* as a guide.

Our initial meetings were supercharged.

Seriously, these are some of the fastest story guys I know, with amazingly fluid minds. Because we are a mutual admiration society, and have such respect for each other's work, we are only interested in making great ideas greater, and straightening our story spines. And the fact *your* script isn't *my* script helps.

What is most surprising about this group, though, is that our problems are the same. Despite our professional accomplishments, we are just as likely to go down the road of a bad idea, or not thoroughly figure out what it takes to make a good idea better. Maybe because of our success, too, we are sometimes less inclined as individuals to admit our blind spots to higher-ups, but in a group of peers like this, we are more likely to let our guard down — and our egos — and see a "note" as a plus.

In a recent session, in point of fact, the subject of "getting notes" was the topic. Dean had two projects at two separate studios and was sharing the joy and the pain of...

... the rewrite process.

As we helped Dean prepare for his meetings, we were playing our favorite game, "Guess what they'll say?" This is the world-weary writer's mental jujitsu that tries to anticipate how bad it will get in that room, what really obvious thing in our script or story *won't* be obvious and *must* be made clearer?

But at core was the fear the process makes scripts worse.

As we played this terrible game, we were brought up short by the more experienced members in our group, particularly Dan. *No one is trying to wreck your script!* was his steadying advice. Having been on both sides of the table, both as a writer getting notes on *Meatballs* and *Stripes* from the legendary Ivan Reitman, and now as a producer himself giving notes to writers, Dan has more experience than any of us. So much of learning is told in stories, and Dan has told us about his experiences writing the classic Bill Murray comedies — and how many blind alleys had to be gone down, and trees slain, in order to get what wound up on screen that seemed, in the end, so simple — and simply great.

No, no one is *purposely* trying to wreck your script!

But since getting and giving notes is about communicating ideas — and since we all see different movies as influences — this is where the pushmi-pullyu that is the script development process sometimes earns that reputation.

When we had finished our work one afternoon, I asked My Guys for a little feedback on how they approach the challenge. How do they negotiate the rewrite process, both as writer, and in Dan's case as producer, to see the world from the executive's point of view?

How have we gotten through the challenge of hearing notes, responding to them, and delivering a script that is still ours?

And what are the benefits of possibly altering the current methods of script development in the future by replacing the "top-down" model (in which executives dictate notes to writers) with a "peer-to-peer" model (like the one we use in our writers groups)?

In either case, success starts with the right attitude.

GOING INTO THE MEETING

You are about to attend your first notes session for a script you've just sold. You're still getting the confetti and champagne out of your hair, and now it's time to face the Muzak. You've heard hints ever since the sale that "of course, there're some improvements" to be made to the script, which now may or may not have devolved into rumors of "a page one rewrite." Since "the day begins the night before," it's a good idea to re-read your script and get up to speed. But in terms of making notes on what you want to fix... don't. Wait. Depending on your deal, you'll likely have at least one more crack at this (**a draft and a set** is the term most often used to describe a rewrite and a polish).

So relax.

The players in the meeting can be any combination of producer, producer's development executive, studio executive assigned to this project, and a clutch of assistants who will one day be executives — so be very nice to them! Usually your ally is the producer who is the "champion" of the project, but he only gets paid once the movie is in production. Besides you, the producer has most to gain. He has twelve more of these projects around town, and is usually, but not always, the best dressed.

After an initial discussion about hybrid cars, you begin.

Yes, everyone loves your script. Yes, they might even love you. But you're here to "write it into production." In truth, as exciting as it is to make a spec sale, the real A-list writers are the ones studios turn to who can fix problems. And often, if you are the original writer, this is the test: Can you stay on? Can you hear notes and deliver what's requested? Or are you going to reveal yourself to be nothing more than the guy who came up with the concept, and thank you very much, there's the door.

If this is your first time selling a script, take some advice from Ben Frahm. Ben is that guy who grabbed the brass ring. He came up with, wrote, and sold a big spec script. Due to the sale and his skill at creating other winning movie ideas (Ben has a true gift for concept), he got an agent at CAA, and is repped by Underground Management, who nurtured the project. But the #1 thing was doing a great job on the rewrite:

> In looking back at my studio notes from Universal for *Dr. Sensitive*, I would offer fellow writers that it's always important to **stay positive** about the project. No matter what happens, keep your head up, and keep working hard. It is so important for writers, especially young writers, to prove to everyone — in particular those at the studio level — that you are a hard-working professional, and totally committed to the project!

There are other situations where that attitude really helps. Perhaps you have been asked to revive a stalled project. Your "take" has been vetted, and now you're here to make sure all agree before sending you off to write. There is also the situation when you have been brought on to write for an **element** — an actor or a director — who wants changes. This is the situation I was in rewriting *Big, Ugly Baby!* for Henry Selick (*Coraline, Nightmare Before Christmas*), though just talking to Henry was privilege enough. Whatever the problem, you're here to fix it. And as you'll hear many times: "You're the writer!" — a refrain that begins to grate almost immediately.

WHAT'S WRONG?

Surprise, surprise: Your work is not done. But what is the headline? What are the main one, two, or three most urgent concerns to address in this new draft? Often, a group consensus has formed before you walked in the door. We've all agreed: That character, section, whole act, or subplot has got to go or be improved. Now it's just a matter of explaining it to you. And Dan has advice for executives — informed by his years as a writer:

> Don't give written notes... at least not before having a meeting to discuss the notes. As a writer, I have never, ever, not had an extreme visceral angry reaction to reading notes from a studio, no matter how eventually good and succinct they

turned out to be. I think it has something to do with the impersonal and cold nature of it — as if these notes are written in stone. There is very little nuance to notes that can naturally occur in a face-to-face meeting.

I tell my producing team: Do your homework. Go over the script and make notes of your feelings on your first read, places that the script lags, or places that really work. **Don't worry about having solutions to the problem areas.** That is open for discussion. You will be surprised how something can be solved in a way that was unexpected. In the face-to-face meeting with the writer(s), first go over general sweeping feelings on the script as a whole. Be frank, but emphasize that everything is up for grabs. It is a discussion, not a list of demands.

After the general discussion, where everyone is encouraged to talk in generalities, go through the script page by page, with everyone giving their thoughts on specific areas. It is also best when there is someone who can stop annoyingly nit-picky notes from getting out of hand, so you can move on to the next topic.

Unfortunately, the result of getting poor, conflicting, or confusing notes, as Dean points out, can lead to problems:

The notes that are less specific are what cause trouble. They have to do with "broadening the audience," making it "four-quadrant," "castable," "edgy," and "less earnest." The last round of notes I received were amusing. Eight pages of **contradicting notes** that called for the script to be all things to all people. "We love the mystery element. Let's fill it with complex twists and nail-biting turns." "Let's make the mystery take a back seat to the blossoming relationship." That kind of thing, page after page. For me, the toughest part of a rewrite is **extracting the actual note from the suggestion(s)** and finding a way to address it within the complex workings of the story. It demands a lot of planning because of the trickle-down effect of every alteration.

As the writer, in addition to getting notes on every page that needs fixing — little things mostly — you must decipher what the main problems are by making sure you understand what is required. At every step of the way, as Dean points out, execs may have different, even contradictory, opinions. That's fine. Nobody's perfect. We're all searching for the solution here and circling the answer isn't an exact science (although using *Save the Cat!* comes close). But since "you're the writer," it's up to you to "get it." If you don't understand, get clarification before starting. If a note is contradictory, without playing "Gotcha!" say so, but only in trying to be clear about what's being asked.

THE INEVITABLE AWKWARD PAUSE

There will sometimes be tension. And the more tension, the more difficult it is to hear notes on your script without having one of two reactions: "I suck" or "You suck," when in truth neither is correct. I have been in meetings, both as the writer and as the producer, when a note is given that a writer disagrees with, resulting in a quite obvious "bile-rising clenching of the teeth," that instant where we all go: *Uh-oh*.

The truth is if you didn't have passion for a project, you would be worth nothing. Studios don't want zombie note takers, but they don't want hair-trigger bomb throwers either. Yet it all starts with that moment in the meeting when someone broaches a subject that the writer does not look happy about. You wanted to call a character Minnie in honor of your favorite grandmother, and the note is: "Kill Minnie." Or worse: "Can we change Minnie's name? She sounds like a mouse." Little darlings like these are dropping left and right, and that's just the warm-up. The whole reason for writing this script is the theme you struggled to build into every scene — "No man is an island" — to which everyone says: "Can we lose the maudlin stuff?"

This is not the theater where the writer's power is supreme; this is not even publishing, where you own the copyright. This is da movies. And in some cases, you are now a hired gun assigned to kill someone you love very much: you. Dan has great advice:

Don't be defensive. I know you've worked months on every word and scene, but the meeting with the producers has to be open-minded about the project as a whole. This is tough, but if you are defending every note, not only will it wear the producers down and make them more reluctant to be even more direct about their feelings, but you won't get a clear picture of their thoughts.

And that is really the job!

But I do have some good news: The more you do this, the easier it becomes — especially after you learn to be open to suggestions. I often think about something that happened years ago with a pair of writers I worked with. Now a successful team, at the time they were young and still finding their stride. On this particular project, we had to deal with several rounds of notes from producers and the team's attitude was unreceptive. The producers were afraid the writers weren't up to the task, and because I was the intermediary, it was my duty to lower the boom. I felt it was not only a defining moment in the project, but in their careers, and told them so, yet had little confidence they heard me.

But at the next meeting, it was like a switch was flipped. The producers' notes were comprehensive, yet the duo didn't hesitate. They went into the rewrite with gusto, and projected the attitude they could be back tomorrow, throw that script out, and start over with even better stuff. The project survived, but more important, I'll always think of it as the moment they turned pro.

To quote Dan:

Don't be afraid to try sweeping changes. You've always got the first draft to fall back on if the second turns out to be too extreme. I can't tell you how many times I've received a second draft where the writer goes on and on about all the changes that were made, only to find that minimal things were done — a few scenes moved around, a character's name changed, whatever. Again, don't be afraid to rewrite stuff, or at least explore big dramatic changes. At least for a day or two.

And I couldn't agree more.

You've heard "writing is rewriting"? Ha! This is child's play compared to the true "*reeee-eee*-writing" we are often called on to perform as screenwriters at the behest of those we've been hired by. And the pros, the winners, the A-listers... don't whine. They just do it. The shooting script for *Little Miss Sunshine* was number 100 according to its author, Michael Arndt. Even in my own experience with *Blank Check*, a movie Colby Carr and I wrote in March of 1993 and was out in theaters by February 1994 (under a year), we had 20 to 30 drafts to get it into shape by first day of shooting, including working through drafts from other writers who had been hired (unbeknownst to us) by the studio. And yet we kept managing to put it back right — and kept improving it, too.

Point is, let go. Get over yourself. You'll always have Paris and that first draft, but if you want to get into production, you have to let those who are responsible for the finances see all the extrapolations of your story they want to. They want the "hero-is-a-teenager" draft when, in fact, the hero in your script is 30 years old? You will try like hell to talk them out of it. But "at the end of the day," it's their dime. To quote Jeremy on this subject:

> Know what fights to fight and when to lay down. If you're 100% sure you are right, fight the fight. If not, then try with your best efforts and who knows, maybe the guy is a big-time producer because he's not such an idiot after all. I've been certain that I was correct about something until I tried it differently and it was better!

INTERPOLATING NOTES

Weaving your way through the rewrite process is about hearing notes and delivering script improvements to the best of your ability. Often this involves "interpolating" to get to the "real note," which can drive writers batty. Yet we must abide.

Once, Colby Carr and I got the feedback that we should make our script "25% funnier." Excuse me? Let me get my Gag-o-meter. But as maddening as that sounds, I actually understood. There were funny bits but there weren't enough of them, *so give me some more of those* — which we did! The other mysterious note in this category had us baffled for a long time. "Too broad" was the note we got. Too broad? Did that mean the scene lapsed into the unbelievable? Was "too broad" short for "not real"? Because we had a lot of "not real" scenes and jokes in our story, and the studio seemed to like *those!* It took us awhile, but we finally figured it out. Too broad meant... "not funny!" It meant: "Doesn't work."

And that's kind of a clue for every note a writer gets. If you want to get binary about it, at its most simple, any red flag offered by any reader or executive means "doesn't work." How or why it doesn't work almost doesn't matter. It just means that the line or scene or character, as it is currently written, stopped the reading process, stopped the enjoyment of the story, and, that in and of itself, must be addressed. I've even talked to writers who are convinced a specific page note — for example, a problem on page 35 — might be about problems that happened several pages before. We may have started to lose the reader five or 10 pages back, so it isn't a bad idea to review the run-up to the actual note to see if the problem doesn't really lie earlier on.

Other little notes that I've heard over the years include:

▶ *Dial it up* or *Dial it down* — Often these phrases are heard in context of minor characters. Can we "dial up" the essence of that character and see or hear more? Can we get more scenes with him or her and make that role bigger? Or, conversely, can we "dial down" to make that character less so? In *Star Wars*, they "dialed up" Yoda as the "prequels" unfolded, but "dialed down" Jar Jar Binks. (If only it was done at the script stage!)

▶ *Too soft* — This was a note — particularly given to me as a family-film writer — that was often baffling. "Too soft" went hand in hand with the notion that my script had to be more "edgy." Too soft meant so sweet or homespun we need insulin shots to read it. But "too soft" can also mean the hero is passive, that there is not enough conflict, or the tone is out-of-date for the audience.

▸ *In your face* — Here's another peculiar one. I was once told that a scene someone felt was dull or not "big" enough, had to be more "in your face." My best guess is this means we need the conflict to be greater, and whatever confrontation was on display — either as a whole or in a scene — had to have more to it. Again, it boils down to: If it "doesn't work," our job is to make it work... or be prepared for executives to hire a writer who will!

LOGIC POLICE

One of my favorite aspects of the rewrite process — and working with others — is the frequent discussion that comes up about **"What would *really* happen?"** We bring different experiences to the development of any script, but it's amazing, no matter how wildly different we are, our sense of "natural law" is the same. And yet finding that consensus can lead to some memorable discussions.

Often these debates occur between notes sessions. We'll have a "tools-down" moment when everyone shares their personal philosophies about a fictional situation, and the different notion of what is logical as we see it. These conversations, examples of which follow, can be remarkable.

What is "justice"? Let's say we're figuring out the punishment for a minor character in a story. Think of the one Jason Alexander plays in *Pretty Woman*. Toward the end of that film, jealous Jason attempts to rape Julia Roberts, and as his just desserts he is denied the friendship of — and a business deal with — Richard Gere. But should he have been more harshly dealt with? What about filing charges? What about reporting his behavior to his wife or his boss? Is Jason's punishment enough?

This same debate can be applied to another favorite example from the Val Kilmer-starring, Martha Coolidge-directed comedy, *Real Genius*. At the end of that film, Kent (Robert Prescott), the Cal Tech "snitch," is implanted with a microchip in his fillings that makes him think God is talking to him, and directing him to help our heroes best the bad guys. His punishment is the "justice" of exclusion and embarrassment. But for a whole movie's worth of nasty things that Kent did to Val and his genius-IQ buddies — including sabotaging a vital experiment — is this enough? When Kent's nearly killed by a satellite laser beam in the Finale, and our heroes rush to save him, should they? Or does Kent deserve to die?

Real Genius: Before he was Batman, Val Kilmer was a Real Genius up against the Big Snitch on Campus, Kent. But does Kent deserve to die?

What is "admirable"? One of my favorite examples of "Save the Cat!" is when we first meet the title character in *Aladdin*, as the hungry waif steals some bread. He's let off the hook for his crime by giving his hard-earned prize to two orphans in an alley — thus "saving the cat." We are even shown Aladdin's sidekick, Abu the monkey, selfishly eating *his* stolen pita, and note the difference between them: Heroes not only have honor, but also the self-control their own pals lack! There's a very different "Save the Cat!" moment in *The Dark Knight*, when we meet Batman battling look-alikes and killer dogs. The "Save the Cat!" beat comes when Batman snaps the neck of one of the dogs — and the audience cheers! Are they right to? Does this show the same compassion that heroes in these kinds of movies are known for? And if not, why are we still rooting to see Batman defeat the Joker? Is it only because the Joker is "worse"? Well, what's worse than strangling a dog?

What is "proper"? Once during a notes meeting for a movie script a partner and I had written, we had a discussion about the hero who had just been stood up by his girlfriend. What should be our guy's response? The reactions around the table were kinda tame, varying from "Call the girl and find out what happened" to "Go to her apartment to see if she's okay." Finally during a pause in the proceedings, a male producer shouted: "Dump the bitch!" to which everyone responded in horror.

On the surface, our reaction to the note was a reaction to him. *Chauvinist! Sexist! Gold-chain-wearing Hollywood producer!* we all were secretly thinking. But in fact what he was pointing out... made sense. What he was *really* saying was that in his opinion he lost respect for a character that didn't stand up for himself. Having been dissed, having been put down by being stood up, maybe being understanding wasn't "proper" at all? It also spoke to a problem we'd been having all along: Our hero was soft (there's that word again), and while that's okay in a rom-com — when the hero is a goofy loser about to learn that his gal is cheating on him — that wasn't the case in this story. In fact, what might be "proper" in a real life situation wasn't appropriate here either!

The real question to ask in all these cases is "What would really happen... *in this world?*" and the answer can be different depending on the type, tone, and subject of each movie. In each of the instances cited above, the solutions are in fact right on. Are the punishments "just" for both Jason Alexander and "Kent"? Yeah, pretty much, given the world of each. Are the "Save the Cat!" beats right for both Aladdin *and* Batman? Considering the tone of each movie, I'd say absolutely; after all, the word "Dark" is in the title of the latter film — what did you expect?

We all walk into the movie theater with a basic notion of the Golden Rule, but it's not always one size fits all. The only thing we ask for as an audience is continuity. The rules of every movie can be different so long as they stay consistent. And enforcing the laws of your movie is a job for the "Logic Police." When they're called in, they must assess on a case-by-case basis.

When the Logic Police do arrive on the scene of any script in progress, they must check in often to make sure we get and stay on course. This is where the "group grope" can help — with insight coming from a source you might not ever have expected; sometimes God inspires our writing and sometimes it's a producer in the corner with a headache who just wants to go home early.

HITTING THE WALL: QUICK FIXES FOR JARRING YOU LOOSE

Invariably in any rewrite process we will "hit the wall." It's not working. We can't quite tell why. And we've been over it again and again till we've worn a hole in the carpet from pacing.

Here are some ways that have worked for me — and for my writers group pals — to break out of the dead end you seem to be in:

▶ *Ask the question!* — In the movie *JFK*, while perusing the Warren Report, a frustrated Kevin Costner as District Attorney Jim Garrison, says: "Ask the question! Ask the question!" There is an elephant in the room, a glaring omission of truth, and yet no one is addressing it. This blindness occurs in screenwriting too. Let's say your story involves a heroine: She's a cop. Her Mom died. Her Dad's her best friend. Well, because we thought this up, that's the way we see it, and that's all we see. All's fine except the drama is flat. Well, take a breath, and... ask the question: Why did she become a cop? How did Mom die? Is Dad dating anybody? Is she? These obvious questions sometimes jar loose an obvious answer — one that's been missing from the story.

▸ *Don't force "logic"* — Often we cling to a Rube Goldberg-like series of story plot points that supposedly pay off. But at what cost? To get our hero to trigger the metal detector he's going through in the airport scene we love, we give him a steel plate in his head received from his tour in Desert Storm — and maybe throw in a great scene with his Draft Board just to make sure we've set it up. But is this a character beat or are we just clinging to the airport scene and the funny line the security guard says? Yes, it all makes sense, but don't go down an unnecessary path.

▸ *Pull the pin* — What is your greatest fear? It's the fear you have to start over. If you pull the pin, the house of cards collapses, so you resist out of — hate to say it! — sheer laziness. That fear of pulling the pin and watching all your hard work be "ruined" is what's constipating you. Well, pull the pin. Blow it up. Then a funny thing happens. When you start picking up the pieces, you may only save one or two, but it might be the ones you can build on in the rewrite. Part of all this is task avoidance, and neither writer nor producer can hold back. Seeking the right answer often involves a radically new idea. To quote Dan again:

> Don't be afraid of non-conventional solutions to problems. Producers, I know you have to eventually present the script to someone higher up, but don't be closed to letting the writers at least try something that might feel too weird. It might just work. Just make it clear that if it doesn't deliver what it should, you will have to find another solution. **Fear is not a friend to creativity.** Let the writers go away and think about all the things that have been discussed and come back to

> pitch which notes work for them and which do not (and possible solutions to problem areas). It is a process... and possibly most important... and I'm not sure how exactly to suss this... **make sure you are on the same page with the writers.** I can't tell you how many times writers have walked away from a meeting and didn't have a clue (or passive aggressively ignored) what the big notes were.

Actually, not to contradict Dan, but I think fear can be a tremendous boost to creativity! As I will talk about in the final chapter, having your back to the wall is often just what the doctor ordered to wring out the very best from a creative person. There's nothing like a little 3:00 a.m. panic to find your focus. I think what Dan really means is "*oppression* is not a friend to creativity." If there is any sense in "that room" that it's "my way or the highway" on the part of executives, or we are not open to something new in the rewriting of a script, it always takes the joy out of it for me as the writer. I have to feel that we're all at least kinda on the same page.

But sadly that is not always the case...

DIFFERENT VISIONS

There are some times in a rewrite when you simply have "creative differences" — a Hollywood term for "*Here are some lovely parting gifts....*" My experiences have mostly been great and I personally have only once walked away from a project — and wished I hadn't. The key is to remain ethical, reasonable, and professional at all times — or at least in public — and not withdraw for any reason that is petty, personal, or piqued. We live to fight another day!

Are there sad stories? Dean has one we've all experienced:

> My script had a "flashing" green light and the studio's full support, including an announcement from the Chairman that it was "exactly the kind of movie we need to be making right now." And then it all reversed with one exec's botched pitch to the CEO. Suddenly, the script was riddled with

flaws and no one, least of all the producers, stood up for it. The project went into a tailspin, the script was rewritten to disheartening studio response, and put into turnaround. It showed me the importance of a good producer and taught me a valuable lesson about the random elements in play in the studio system — none of which you can anticipate or control. There's a definite luck element to it all.

There is many a slip twixt the green light and the script, but we have no choice but to keep plugging away. To quote Jeremy:

No retreat, baby! No surrender! Don't quit! Keep trying! Keep pushing! Go down a direction even if it's the "wrong" one. You never know when a director or actor will come on and want to go back to the original direction, so stay with the project until you're ready to throw up from everyone asking: "How's (fill in title here) doing?" Make them force you to quit, but never jump!

If only there were another development solution...

A NEW HOPE

One of the reasons my producer pal Dan was attracted to the *Save the Cat!* method of our workshops is because it's an alternative to the current development track. As stated, the top-down model (screenwriter being given notes by executives) might benefit from the success of the peer-to-peer model found in our small group. In fact, Dan's interest in our group dynamic was piqued further once we saw how effective it was. There was even a call to take our act on the road as a kind of traveling notes-giving machine, offering the collective feedback of seasoned pros to anyone whose script needs help.

But the needs of our own careers came first.

And yet this peer-to-peer model continues to fascinate.

When asked to do a retreat for animators at a major studio in 2009, I was prepped by a remarkable article from *Harvard Business Review* titled "How Pixar Fosters Collective Creativity," by Ed Catmull, about the Pixar development model that works along these same lines. With maybe the most astounding series of hits in movie history, from *Toy Story* and *The Incredibles* through *Wall-E* and *Up*, Pixar must be doing something right in vetting, refining, and rewriting scripts in progress.

Pixar calls it Peer Review, in which a director and a writer working on a project can meet with a panel of seasoned greats (including John Lasseter and Brad Bird), who hear stories in progress. Yet writers are not ordered to include their boss's suggestions — and aren't guaranteed that including them will win approval. In a weird way, it's just like our workshops: With no vested interest in your project, other than as a creative puzzle, ideas flow more easily and with greater objectivity. And I can tell you from our group that the projects Dean, Ben, Dan, Jeremy, and I worked on got better geometrically, and led directly to sales… and green lights. What about this model can be used in taking and giving notes, and what about it is really different?

Part of what makes peer-to-peer work is lack of emotional attachment. Both in our own writing groups, and in the peer review dynamic, it's your story, and you are the one ultimately responsible for it. And our panel, the group who is listening to your struggle as you pitch out the beats, or breathlessly hand us your latest draft, have one thing you don't have: apathy. Reading your script or hearing your pitch, we're just bystanders. We're listening or reading and responding like any audience would.

So, what are our rules of engagement? And how can we utilize them in the context of a peer-to-peer style review?

THE 50 QUESTIONS

Believe it or not, we can critique without being critical. And we can take our own prejudices out of the development process in favor of universal truths we can count on.

We start by asking questions. I've come up with 50 — from the initial idea through every phase of the script — that get to the heart of all script-development issues. If you honestly answer these questions about your own project, or anyone's, odds are you will come out way ahead.

The diagnostic review is the "greenlight" checklist that keeps us all from playing a game we can't win — whether we're the writer or the producer.

And because I always start with an "Atta boy," finding at least one thing done well from the last draft, we'll start asking questions at a much higher level:

You worked hard. You are a tad frazzled.

Well, I'm here to tell you, you're great.

And we're going to make you, and your script, even greater!

Save the Cat! Greenlight Checklist

Title
> ▸ Is this the best title to tell us what this story is visually and emotionally? Does it "say what it is"?

Pitch logline
> ▸ Can you pitch this in a minute?
> ▸ Is what you pitch being delivered in the script?
> ▸ Does it grab the audience and keep them wanting more?

Mini-story logline
> ▸ Can you easily tell your story through its key beats?

ACT I
Opening Image
> ▸ Does the **tone** tell us what kind of story this is without giving away too much?
> ▸ Does the Opening Image put us in the right **mood** for the **type** of movie it is?
> ▸ Do we get a clear picture that this Opening Image is the "**before**" shot?

Theme Stated
> ▸ Is there a **thematic premise** being raised?
> ▸ Do we know what this story will be about **on the inside**?
> ▸ Is it **primal** for all audiences?

Set-Up
- Do we know who the **hero** of the story is?
- Is this hero **as far back as possible** when we first meet him/her?
- Is the hero and his/her world rife with **problems**? What are they and are they clear?

Catalyst
- Is something **done** to our hero?
- Does it force our hero into **action**?
- Is it **believable**?

Debate
- Is there a valid **argument** for the hero?
- Is it the hero who has the **debate**?
- Does it give us insight into the hero's **emotions**?

ACT II

Break into Two
- Is it a clear act break that tells us our hero is moving into a **new world**?
- Did the hero make a **proactive** choice to move into Act Two?
- Does the hero have a **clear goal** as he/she enters Act Two?

B Story
- **Who** or **what** is the B Story?
- Does the B Story have a **spiritual lesson** to teach the hero?
- Does it provide a needed **breakaway** from the A Story?

Fun & Games
- Does it show the **promise of the premise**?
- Do we have enough **set pieces**?
- Is there a **touchstone scene** that defines what this movie is all about?

Midpoint
▸ Is there a clear **false victory** or **false defeat**?
▸ Are the **stakes raised**? Is there a **time clock**?
▸ Is there a **public outing** or a **party** that exposes our hero and forces him/her to declare his/her new way of being?

Bad Guys Close In
▸ Does the quest become **harder** for the hero?
▸ Are there enough **external** and **internal forces** attacking the hero? What is the **awful truth** the hero cannot admit?
▸ Do we see the hero being **stripped of** his/her **comfort zone** one piece at a time?

All Is Lost
▸ Is there a **whiff of death**, physically or emotionally?
▸ Does it feel like the hero's **lowest point**?
▸ Is the All Is Lost as **devastating** a blow to the hero as we can make it? And what is his **shard of glass**?

Dark Night of the Soul
▸ Does the hero **confess** his/her flaw, secret, or ugly truth, and have a **moment of clarity**?
▸ Does the B Story **prompt** our hero into Act 3?
▸ Is the Theme Stated **re-enunciated** at this point?

ACT III

Break into Three
▸ Is it a **clear** act break?
▸ Does the hero **move** the story through the act break?
▸ Does our hero have a **new goal**?

Finale
▸ Is there a **storming of the castle** which our hero leads?
▸ Is the Act 3 world the **synthesis** of Act 1 and Act 2 worlds?
▸ Is the **B Story** clearly resolved?

Final Image
- ▸ Is it the **opposite** of the Opening Image?
- ▸ Do we get a real sense of **transformation** for our hero?
- ▸ Is this the **right way** to end the story?

Raising the Bar:
- ▸ Does every scene move the plot forward through conflict and emotional shifts?
- ▸ Do all the minor characters play a key role in our hero's growth, and do they change and learn a lesson as well?
- ▸ Is there any line, scene, or character that is cliché, and is there any place where we can push what is expected?
- ▸ What is new about this movie and, given its genre, does it move the art forward?
- ▸ Who is this movie for and does the script do anything that veers from that target audience?

As we get better at reading scripts and giving notes to others, this checklist becomes second nature. The idea of it is only to make the rewrite process less like hell and more like heaven. Because here's a surprise: With the right input, rewriting can be heavenly — if you know the process isn't about wrecking your vision, but bringing out your best!

As long as you are willing to strike back, you, too, can win! And over time, as I've become a veteran of this process, it becomes all about doing it again... and again!

Yes, a lot of our business is about repetition, and there is no greater example of that good habit in action, than successfully selling your script... and yourself.

So let me introduce a slogan I first heard at the Alameda Writers Group, which I adhere to, and hope will soon be yours:

Write. Sell. Repeat.

chapter 6

CLOSE ENCOUNTERS OF THE SELLING KIND

Blake's Blog /
April 24, 2008

"As we look out on the landscape, the more specific we can be, the better. When we target our careers and our scripts, we see a vision that becomes the truth, so it's important to pick well. And dream big."

Oh! The joy! The splendor! that is selling a script.

It always seems so easy once it happens.

Colby Carr and I spent the days leading up to our spec sales telling each other: "*Someone* has to buy this, don't they?" — a mantra we hoped would be a self-fulfilling prophecy.

And very often, it was.

We'd done the work, turned our well-written 110-page screenplay over to our agent, were totally confident... and yet there was always that nagging doubt: Would anybody buy it?

As the spec sale began to unfold, and the bids started coming in, I still felt like we'd beaten long odds. It was on days like these, with multiple offers competing for our team's approval, when you had to restrain me from driving down Wilshire Boulevard past Agency Row in Beverly Hills and whooping out loud:

"That's right! I'm *baaaad!*"

Because when a sale sticks and you're "in" — oh, man!

The one-day spec sale is a rarer animal these days. Yes, it happens, and discovering the intersection of Art and Commerce never fails to be a rush. Whether it takes one day or several weeks to get a script "out to the town," the process is the same.

So how do I get in on it, you ask?

Some of you are just starting and are sure it's about "who you know." Others have sampled success, but wonder, after being lost in the desert lo these many years, if you will ever again drink the rejuvenating waters that can only come with a "Yes!"

For until that shining day, we are all in the wilderness.

The trip to the Promised Land took Moses 40 years. If you look at a map, it's an 11-day journey. What was the hold-up? Why did Moses meander for decades when the end point was staring him in the face? The answer is the same for all who assay a goal. For as important as it is to envision success, and even more important to take steps to secure it, it is every bit as vital — however you will it into being — that you believe success can be yours.

Because that is key.

You will get here, I swear. But one thing I know for sure: A sale is just the beginning of securing a career.

And it all starts with saying: *I can have this!* out loud.

THE AGENT WILL APPEAR!

In the beginning was the Word.

But very soon after that, the Word had to get an agent.

Let's call it "spreading the Word," because that's what agents do. And that's what this chapter's about: getting you out of despair and into the sales zone, and casting a new light on the selling process — hopefully with a check at the other end.

While having an agent is key to that — and I cannot stress enough the importance of finding one who can position you and your script and continue working with you to raise you to the level of greatness you deserve — let's not get ahead of ourselves. Right now you may not have an agent, and I'm here to tell you:

That's okay.

I've said it before, and I'll say it again: You may think the lack of an agent is what's stopping you; you will say to yourself: "If only..." and let it be a barrier. But I hope to calm writers whenever they veer into a rant about representation by telling them this truth:

An agent is not the most vital thing on your to-do list.

Can an agent change your life? You betcha. Can the right agent pull off miracles for you that will elevate you to great heights? Absolutely. But here's a shocker: I have never, ever, gotten any job, or sold any script, without doing my part first.

And that goes for you, too.

Lately, I not only get to cite the experiences of long-time veterans like myself, but also tell you about new writers like Ben Frahm who have shown me a thing or two when it comes to the guts it takes to win. To be honest, I rely on Ben's experiences quite a bit, for they prove two things beyond a whisper of doubt:

1. Like me, Ben is a go-getter with a positive attitude and a drive for success. Yes, that still works! And...

2. ... Nothing's changed. Yes, the business is different, the sales less spectacular. But we can all still win!

Ben and others like him prove that if you follow the steps I suggest, you too have a shot at success — still! —*always!*

I hope Ben's example inspires you as much as it does me.

I first met Ben after he moved to L.A. fresh from Cornell University, discovered my first book, and emailed me. I suggested he come to one of my early workshops, those wild and woolly days when we tried to work out all 40 beats in one weekend. After Ben recovered, and followed the procedure I recommended for getting his script to interested parties once it was completed, he was contacted by Underground Management, which has a long track record of successfully working with new writers and getting them careers. But it wasn't until another production company expressed interest in Ben — which Ben let Underground know about — that their eagerness to step up and commit to working with him came about.

I still marvel at what Ben did. As I suggested, Ben sent 100+ queries to agents, managers, and production companies in the *Hollywood Creative Directory*. He got about 4 or 5 responses back (a fairly good return, believe it or not), but it was enough to let this bright kid parlay one firm against another to make sure they knew with whom they were dealing. Was he fair? Absolutely! Was he honest and forthright? Totally. But he knew what he wanted. And because he had taken our workshop and had feedback from others about the project he was pitching...

He also knew what he had.

And yet, Ben's journey was just beginning.

No, Underground did not sign Ben. They instead agreed to work with him on many drafts of *Dr. Sensitive* to get it in shape.

And that took time.

Between multiple rewrites, and Ben's busy work schedule (this young man had a day job as a special-needs teacher at a school here in L.A.), he would call me up and, frankly, whine. Where was this going? Why didn't his newfound managers who loved him so, or said they did, sign him? And the number one complaint on *Ben's Top Ten Greatest Whines* was: Why don't I have an agent?

To which I'd say: *Trust me, Ben, the agent will appear.*

Yet as weeks turned into months, nothing was happening.

So Ben would phone with the same complaint.

Trust me, Ben, I'd repeat, *the agent will appear.*

While driving back from giving a speech at the Great American Pitchfest here in Los Angeles, my cell phone rang. It was Ben with news: Universal just bought his script, and guess what?

What!?

Ben had an agent! Seems just before going out with the script, Underground got Ben a really great rep from CAA who had handled the whole thing. She was standing right there by his side the whole time — and even negotiated a better deal for him!

Imagine that.

I don't mean to sound smug, but this is just part of the grow-ing-up process we all must do with our careers. Agents don't appear on hope. They don't appear because you're a nice guy or gal with a great idea and a lot of promise. They appear when there's something real for them to appear for, that allows them to do what *they* do best, namely take the interest that is already there in a finished property and pound the buyer into making a better deal for their client. And until those things are in place, not only is there no need for an agent, but thinking about getting one is a distraction to the job at hand:

Writing a great script.

The real irony of all this is the fact that after the first blush of success was over, and Ben had completed his rewrites for Universal and was ready for the next step, he got another surprise. There he was, remember, with both a manager *and* an agent — and all top people in the business, by the way.

And being what it is, along with an agent, an attorney had also appeared. *Wouldn't you know it!* My buddy Ben was now an S Corp with a great name for his company: Picture Frahm Productions, Inc. Yup. There he was. All agented up, and rarin' to go! So when he walked into CAA wearing his new Prada loafers (no tassels — that's for East Coast squares), got his complimentary bottle of Fiji water, and was seated at the right hand of his agent, he was expecting a wand to be waved over him; instead he got a question:

"So Ben," said his ten-percenter. "What're you working on?"

I would have loved to be a fly on the wall for that moment. See?

Even with a deal, money in the bank, a record of success, and experience in the trenches, it's only leading to the next level, and the next level is pretty much the same as the first:

Whaddya got for me?

And so it was back to the drawing board. Write. Sell. Repeat. But when Ben returned to work, he did so with the knowledge not only that he was good at this — good enough to get a major-league sale — but that success was up to him.

He knew how to get there.

He will get there again!

And he'll do so with help, but mostly by doing the work.

THE AGENT VS. MANAGER SLAPDOWN

You'll note too in this scenario another sage bit of wisdom I offer new writers in particular that has proven to be a winner: *Forget the agent, start with a manager!* Of all the people Ben queried when he sent out his batch of emails to targets culled from the *Hollywood Creative Directory*, managers were the most likely to respond. Why? Well, because in fact, managers are sometimes what I like to call **stealth producers**. Yes, they are interested in promoting your writing career but they are also interested in "attaching themselves" to your screenplay. And because they are managers — and not agents licensed to represent and sell their client solely — they are perfectly within their right to do so.

To which I add: *You go, Manager-man!*

It may explain the rash of managers (and by rash, I don't mean the dermatological kind) that has broken out of late, and for whom you offer as much opportunity as they offer you.

To be a manager, all you have to say is that you are one. You put up your "shingle" (see *Variety*) and claim you can move projects forward, and get contacts for your clients, and *voila!* You can.

Hopefully.

Yes, there are a lot of folks out there who can rightfully claim to be a manager. And lots who can't. By signing up with one, you are mostly getting someone who wants to be a manager-slash-producer. And if you do your homework, and can vet them with research, I highly recommend it. While they will also be concerned with furthering your career, and can do that too, most are doing so to be involved in your movie.

If a true stealth producer is going to represent you, he must avoid what's called **double dipping**. This is where a manager charges a client both a manager's fee and gets a fee or producer bonus to be attached to your project. This is a no-no. And if your manager says this is perfectly okay, you might drop the phrase "conflict of interest" into the conversation. Yup. If you ever want your phone call returned — and I mean lickety-split — that's the expression you want noted on the while-you-were-out pad on your manager's desk.

The controversy about managers and their true purpose goes on. And yet I insist they offer many advantages due to the ever-changing nature of the business… and a Hollywood in flux. The rise in the number of managers has come about because they are filling a need. There are more writers hoping for spec gold; there are also more ways to sell projects — Indie, Direct to DVD, Made for Cable, webcast, TV movie — and not enough agents to cover it all. Agents cannot live on 10% of a tiny Direct-to-DVD sale; neither can a manager based solely on his fee. But someone has to push, and to do so there has to be more reward for the pusher; thus the stealth producer has a role to fill.

It's also because the role of agent is different. In the old days, the agent worked for… me, the writer. And while that's still the case, more and more agents represent "the project." Why? Same thing. Economics. As an agent, I am less interested in your unsold one-act play, or your Indie-oriented "small" film, as I am in the thing I can pick up the phone and get an answer on today. I also think that because studios develop less, and are looking for "ready-to-shoot" scripts and projects that are easy to set up, the agent has become the *de facto* Story Department. Agents work for their clients, of course, and help create and launch projects their clients are working on, but they are more like gatekeepers for studios that don't develop as they used to.

And again, all that's fine; just be aware.

These days, I personally have just a manager, my bud, Andy Cohen, and we too work on a project-by-project basis. Sometimes Andy will take a manager's fee and sometimes he will attach himself to a project, and by doing so, ensure that I and my script are better represented when the movie is made. It's only when we need an agent to sell a project that we seek one out.

If I were new to the business, I might follow Ben Frahm's lead and "agent up" with a manager, agent, and lawyer. Contrariwise, I know some writers that use just a lawyer to close deals — or even do the negotiating themselves. Whatever works for you, do it. But when starting out, we are looking for partners, and very often that comes with the price of being managed or "magented," a term coined by manager Christopher Pratt.

Yes, the agent vs. manager question has changed over the years, and will continue to morph based on where you are in your career, and where the business is. But one thing that is true for everyone today is how much work it takes to get a script ready for market. It's why you hear so many stories of representatives asking clients to do rewrites before sending a script out. And I don't mean polishes, I mean *reeeee-eeeeeee*-writes, often multiple drafts over months. Agent or manager, their reasons are the same:

1. The selling climate for specs is way tougher, and the days of **throwing it over the wall** of a studio are past; scattershot submissions are rarely successful, but more importantly…

2. A half-baked script is bad for the agent's and/or manager's reputation. *Why should I trust you next time you say a piece of material is great… when the last three you sent me were just tragic?*

When it comes to the hours of "free" work it takes to get a script ready, it's up to you. You can stand on your outrage and demand: *Send my script out now! I don't want to do any more rewrites! I am tired of doing your bidding! I'm the writer here!*

But every time I've done that, I'd wished I hadn't.

Ironically, part of the reason to do this work is to get your agent or manager invested in your project. Not only is your rep more in tune with the demands of the market, but if she can take pride in helping you massage a script, even suggesting bits and plot points that work, and you incorporate, just think about it…

Wouldn't you take more care on a sale of something you helped bring to life than on one you have no personal stake in?

It's like Peter Pan says to Wendy as they jump out the window: *You gotta believe!* It's so much better — and we might actually fly — if we're holding hands as we take the leap!

COST VS. RETURN

Among the members of your team — attorney, agent, and manager — all have different interests in your career, and charge different percentages. Typically the range of fees is like this:

Attorney: 5-7%

Agent: 10%

Manager: 10-15%

This may sound like a lot, but it *is* tax deductible! And in my experience, these folks — especially attorneys — are getting you over and above the percentage they are taking, sometimes two or three times that just by their very presence on a deal. And the right team is not only an economic benefit for you, but sleep-better-at-night insurance. How many times have I sat upright in bed at 3:00 a.m. wondering about a particular point on a contract, only to hit the hay five seconds later knowing my guys are the best and have already handled it? What you are buying with your percentages is confidence it's being done right.

Of course, horror stories do exist. I've heard examples where the writer, lawyer, and agent are satisfied with a deal, but the part of the contract we're waiting to close is... the manager's deal! Why? Because the stealth producer has suddenly appeared like Godzilla and wants to be included — or else he'll eat the building. In other cases, I have heard of deals collapsing, or slowed indefinitely, because the lawyer was taking great glee in bashing the lawyer on the other side, and having a grand old time while everyone else waits — but that's what they do.

Lawyers frequently end up as studio executives and have agendas of their own. They are trying to make money for their firms, of course, and make partner if they can. But they are also there for you on other matters, and do work over and above their client's strictly professional needs. They can be hired on an hourly fee, but if hired on a 5-7% basis, they will often handle small personal matters, like minor legal problems and the reviewing of insurance and financial questions.

From the outside looking in, you're wondering, should you get this thing rolling? Is it worth giving away so much?

Hell yes.

Remember it was just you and your subscription to *People* magazine a minute ago. Three times the representation means three times the contacts. Should you spell out your concerns when you first meet with each member of the team? Of course. But if you're sitting across from me and dictating terms of how the deal should go before it happens, I might look askance. I might even put you in the life's-too-short category. Either you vet these folks and trust them or you don't. And remember the advice my wise old dad gave me: *50% of something is better than 100% of nothing.*

THE SWIRLING VORTEX OF HOLLYWOOD

Truth be told, everybody is interested in the same thing: that new and easy project that will boost their careers and bring in a hatful of success — financial, critical, or both. Agents can **package** by adding other clients from their agency, and help their agency get a bigger piece of the pie; managers can do the same, including other clients as well as themselves in your deal; and studio execs are looking for sure bets, easy-to-make projects that will fill the slots of their studio's calendar.

That is, after all, the big difference between Indie and major studio production: Major studios are "programming" slots with say, summer blockbusters (May - September), Oscar contenders (October - December), holiday movies (Valentines Day, July 4, Christmas, Thanksgiving), and dumping "dogs" that got made, cost money, and now must recoup (second half of August and January - February). There is also a "spec sale season" that is usually two times a year: *February 15 to July 1* and *September 1 to December 15.* This is normally when most specs are bought because that's when studio budgets are established for the year — and ready to be spent!

All these people have a whole lot more on their minds than your script, which may or may not be delivering the Fun and Games or have Midpoint problems. Because if it does not deliver... next! That is the swirling vortex of Hollywood. Let them do their jobs; your job is to make sure your script is as perfect as it can be.

And remember:

"This... is the business... we have chosen."

If you want to produce movies or if you're a filmmaker, that's different. But if you're a screenwriter who wants a career with the majors, with rewrites, assignments, and sales, pay heed!

See, the funny thing about the whole circuit is no matter where you are in the hierarchy, no matter how much clout you wield, we're all asking the same question Ben's agent asked:

Whaddya got for me?

Sometimes in my fantasies, I see myself as the head of development somewhere, green-lighting movies and working with writers, directors, and producers to make my projects the biggest hits they can be. But how, really, is that different than everything else I've done in my career? I've forever been the screenwriter who is thinking up posters and writing movies that will please most people most often. It's no different than what everyone on every level is doing all over town. What's that special, sizzling-hot, extra-cool thing that will fill my bill?

Not only for the people in charge, but the public too!

I may be a smart writer — or agent or lawyer or manager — but when someone asks: *How's it going?* what they're really asking is:

Whaddya got for me?

How is whatever you are developing of interest to, and for... me? If it's good, how can I get in on it? If I can't get in on it, how can I learn from what you're doing and make my projects more like yours? The bonus that writers have is they are the ones who can think up and execute these ideas. You as the writer have tremendous power. Don't ever forget that it starts with you.

In the beginning was the Word. And the Word is yours alone!

THE DAILY GRIND

So now you have it all. Scripts in play. Agents and managers at your beck and call. That show biz personal trainer who is taking 10% of your body fat (hopefully). Now what?

Agents will tell you, or tell me anyway, that they will spend the first half of your career "putting you into a box" — and the second half of your career getting you out of it.

What this means is, in order to sell you, they too have to figure out what they're selling and package you accordingly.

If you are a horror writer, it will be easier to sell you, and send you up for assignments, if you are a really good horror writer who specializes in horror and are the go-to guy or gal in... horror. If you are a comedy writer, it will be easier to sell you if you not only write comedy, but specialize further by being a *type* of comedy writer. Do you write spoof, rom-com, gross-out, sophisticated, or urban comedy? Then every assignment that comes up in your category is one I'll send you out on.

My friend Tracey Jackson, whom I've known since I was three — I even have a photo of me, Tracey, and Jamie Lee Curtis at a nursery school birthday party (available upon request) — has always written witty women's comedy. It's why she was hired to adapt *Confessions of a Shopaholic* (2009). Tracey writes "funny women" and "sophisticated" comedy, so if you have a project that falls into these categories, she's one of three or four top women writers in town to call.

In addition, Tracey turned a penchant for all things Bollywood into an original sale of *The Guru* (2000), and now also is asked in every time a Bollywood comedy needs an American twist. And because she is a very smart careerist, Tracey has never been afraid to turn down assignments or reject being put up for ones that aren't in her category. Why? Because she not only knows her strengths and preferences as a writer, she also realizes the loss of focus that comes from being all things to all people.

Point is: By finding a specialty and getting really good at it — or going further and making a category of movie uniquely your voice, e.g., "It's a J.J. Abrams actioner" or "It's a Judd Apatow comedy" — you make it easier to sell you.

How does an agent "put you up" for an assignment?

Well... there's this big book. It's called the **Open Assignments Book**, and all the major agencies maintain one. It's no more than a printout in a binder where every studio and production company that is looking for someone to rewrite an existing script is listed. Don't be horrified if the project you sold as a spec screenplay turns up on this list, because most screenplays go through multiple writers. Especially as the studio gets closer to green-lighting a movie, they will make sure they've done everything they can to get it into optimum shape.

You may also wish to develop other skills. There are writers who specialize in structure; writers who specialize in dialogue or action set pieces; and writers who are called in to do the pass that will simply straighten out all of the other drafts and distill them into the final shooting script.

You've heard, I'm sure, that there are many professional screenwriters who have never had a screen credit who work for decades making a very nice living doing nothing else but such doctoring. These hired guns can be expensive (a one week "pass" on a script by these specialists might run you $500,000 or more). And it all gets back to the vital question I asked myself at a turning point in my career:

What service do I offer?

Am I best at coming up with ideas? Writing a particular type of movie? Or being an expert in one aspect of the writing process?

Finding the thing you do best, and nurturing it, is what a good agent or manager will work with you to exploit.

The ideal, and what most agents/managers recommend, is:

▸ *Do* always be working on a spec or two or three.

▸ *Do* always go up for assignments you're right for, and once you're hired, do your best to "write it into production."

▸ *Do* always be thinking what your service is. What is it you do better than anyone, and how can you develop "a voice" that is uniquely yours?

These three activities will keep you plenty busy. You should never be sitting on your hands, wondering what you should be doing to further your career. Before you call up your agent to bug her (more on that in a minute), you should make sure you're doing everything on this list — because odds are at the end of your chat, it's what your ten-percenter will suggest, too. I know all this sounds like a lot, but it's not. It's your job now.

So say it aloud: *I can do this!* Yes. You can.

PITCHES, REWRITES, AND "GET-TO-KNOW YA'S"

I was being a little facetious when I told you about Ben's meeting with his agent. Yes, the point of the conversation was: *What're you working on?* And you'll always be working on coming up with a spec. But Ben was also offered the chance to meet with people around town by his smart agent — all due to his success.

There was Ben BEFORE, like so many of you, in the desert, just him and his ideas. Now here he was AFTER with his Fiji water, ready to "go to the next level." Pretty cool! Ben had passed the first test. He'd written and sold a script. Now he has to get more projects "in the pipeline," and that means a combination of **Pitches**, **Rewrites**, and **Get-to-Know Ya's**. So what are these?

"Pitches" are just that, a verbal presentation of a script yet to be written, and one reason Ben's agent was asking what he is working on. Having sold a script, Ben is in a much better position to pitch new ideas and perhaps sell them. During the spec screenplay send-out, Ben's agent made a list of possible producers who might be interested. In addition to Underground, another producer was needed to "take the script into the studio." I don't know about

Ben's sale, but an agent may make phone calls to, and send scripts out for, 20 – 50 producers, hoping to ramp up interest in a script. (So you see how much work is involved?) In the course of this, some liked Ben's script, some passed, but even those who didn't sign on may have liked Ben's writing. And having seen someone else ace them out of a sale, they are more inclined now to meet and see what Ben has that might help *them*.

Whaddya got for me?

Pitch meetings are ever thus. If it's a hot idea, or if the writer has "heat," the agent will gang up many meetings in a few days hoping to generate the same kind of excitement a spec sale does. More often, it's a calmer affair. One producer may like the idea most, so more meetings are set to work on the pitch and get it ready for sale.

But it all starts with that initial meeting.

If you are versed in *Save the Cat!* you are ahead of other pitchers. Poster. Logline. Simple story spine. Eager and inspired telling of the tale. Ten minutes, tops. That's the pitch.

One of the handiest hints I've seen to organize your pitch came up in one of my classes in Seattle. Betty Ryan constructed a great way to give a concise outline of her story by identifying seven key points of the BS2 to guide all her pitches:

Betty Ryan's Short Pitch Guide
1. Opening Image – A brief "who" of the hero
2. Catalyst – The thing that sets the story in motion
3. Break into Two – The essence of the story and poster
4. Midpoint – The complication that challenges the hero
5. All Is Lost – How the hero loses everything
6. Break into Three – The solution to the hero's dilemma
7. Final Image – How he is transformed by this story

Regardless of how you organize your story, once you've finished your pitch... shut up! The first one to talk loses. If you give into temptation and can't help spewing more stuff after you've said "The End," you are indulging in a pitching no-no called **Selling Past the Close.** My other advice is, once you've pitched, and waited, and they pass and then ask if you have anything else you'd like to pitch to them... say no. Others will disagree, but to me, I think writers should be more than guys with a coat full of watches. *Don't like that one? How about this?*

I need to believe that what you're pitching me means something to you. You can hint that you have other things you're working on, and thumbnail those, but if they want to hear your next idea, schedule a time to come back in and tell it right.

Rewrites follow the same pattern. Having read Ben, a producer or a studio might have work for him on a stalled script, book, or other project yet to gel. When there is material to review before the meeting, they'll send it to you to prepare. What everyone is looking for is your "take." My advice is to not necessarily listen to what the producers think they want. A stalled project is so because producers keep hearing the same old solutions, so your job is to try to think "outside the brads" of the script, and come up with a fresh take.

Many times the way to do that is to review the very same techniques we've been using on your script — namely "The Five Questions to Straighten the Story Spine" (see Chapter 4) or a review of the "Three Worlds" of a story landscape (see Chapter 3). And when you dazzle them with your skills and get the job, delivering can really help your career. The A-list writers are those that master this service.

"Get-to-know ya's" (also called "Generals") are less formal; if you have a coat full of watches to sell, now's the time to whip 'em out! The producer or executive liked your script. This is her chance to put writer's voice to writer's face. Sometimes, if a General goes well, you'll spark to one of her ideas, or she'll spark to one of yours. These casual meetings can get serious fast.

BEFORE, DURING, AND AFTER THE MEETING

Me? I like to dress nicely for these events. After I prepare, I try to make sure I've got a casual, but professional, outfit ready. Women, I've learned from Tracey, are best served by wearing comfortable chic. Tracey always wears nice slacks and a blouse to our pitches, and always has great personal presence. Tracey is a former actress (you can see her in the hairdresser scene of *Heartburn*) and is "funny in the room" as they say. It helps. If you aren't like this, or feel like you want some tips in this area, read my pal Stephanie Palmer's book, *Good in a Room*, which is excellent. I even keep a diary, a habit I developed early on, and make notes about what projects I'm pitching, whom I met with, what my impressions were about both them and my performance, and make sure I put every contact into a database that I keep updating every year.

I also like to drop a quick written thank you note to the executive I met with. And if there is some news item or hobby we touched on in the meeting that's personal, I usually mention it. Just a friendly letter on the occasion of our meeting!

THE CARE AND FEEDING OF YOUR TINY TEN PERCENTER

The result of every meeting is duly observed and communicated to your agent or manager or lawyer or whoever it is who set it up. If it went badly, they will hear about it; if you tanked the pitch, it will be noted, and the report card of all your strengths and weaknesses filed away for future reference.

It is all about the ongoing relationship with your representatives... and you are keeping tabs on them as well!

Since you have three best friends now — your new friend, the agent; your best bud, the manager; and your most favorite person in the whole wide world, your attorney — there's nothing wrong with keeping all of them on their toes. This is like the checks and balances of the Legislative, Executive, and Judiciary branches in the U.S. Government — though I will not say who is President in our Hollywood configuration. Often I have called up my lawyer when I have a problem with my agent. He then places a call and the problem is resolved. Got a glitch with your lawyer? Talk to the manager about it. He's there to help! Explain why you don't want that codicil added to your contract. It sounds so much better when your manager is telling your attorney than when you do. So let Mr. Stealth Producer know.

All of it is about the forwarding of your career and the generation of material that makes everyone *keep* being interested in you. This speaks to "getting you out of your box," which usually comes when you're mid-career, have had numerous sales, rewrites, and co-ventures with others in your genre, but suddenly the phone stops ringing. You're in your box all right, and now the question becomes: Do you want to be buried in it?

We'll discuss more about this in the next chapter, with the "re-booting" process. Know for now that a good agent or manager will be cognizant of this too, and, like Tracey's Bollywood interest, be ready to expand your options.

Yet it all comes back to you.

It's simple! Your relationship with your agent is about the developing of your creative impulses and letting someone know about these in order to exploit them. There are all kinds of *do's* — three I have noted above. Here are some *don'ts*:

- ▸ *Don't* call up to chat! — If a rep wants a pal to "say hi" or "check in," they will call one. This relationship isn't social; it's business. If you must call, have a point and make it brief. Most of all: Let them call you.

- ▸ *Don't* badmouth your agent — They're family — for now — and talking badly about one's agent only reflects badly on you. Besides, there's no better way to help than to talk your agent up!

- ▸ *Don't* plot against your agent — You may think your little scheme for making a deal will impress your reps; it will only complicate matters. You do your job; let the agent make the sale.

But the number one "don't" I've found to be most helpful in my career and will italicize and even center here in hopes it makes an impact:

Don't... bitch.

Writers are whiners. It goes with the territory. In truth you have only one job: Plant your butt in the chair and write something. It's painful, I know. Occasionally your mind drifts. And what your mind drifts *to*, much of the time is: Why isn't my agent calling? Which leads to the next thought: My agent sucks.

And you are wrong.

Next time you have this thought, do what writer Stephen J. Cannell suggested to a group of writers at the 2008 Final Draft Screenwriting Contest, for which I was a judge. Cannell, who is the world's most successful TV show creator (*The Rockford Files*, *The A-Team*, and a host of others), is now also a prolific novelist, and I note, a family man, married to his high school sweetheart for 40 years. He also labored in the wilderness, one hand clapping, the other one typing, for six long years, getting rejection slips from everyone while he got better at his j-o-b (please stone me if I ever use the word "craft"). Even when he got an agent, and moved his family to Hollywood, he still had a hard time. Though we all know what a powerhouse writer he is now, no one knew it back then.

When Cannell did not get the job, or did not sell the script, he did something remarkable:

He'd take his agent to lunch and thank her.

Thank you for taking me on as your client! I know you are doing everything you can do for me — and I know I'm tough to sell. It's a tough marketplace. But you are the closest person to me in my professional life and I will do everything I can to help you do your job. You are my link to the film community. And I just want you to know I appreciate everything you're doing.

Can you imagine what an agent would do for a client after *that* conversation? Why she'd go out and kill for a guy like that!

So much better than calling up and mincing around, asking why it isn't going better? And why didn't you read that one-act play I sent you, and what about TV? And *bitch, bitch, bitch*.

If this describes you, no wonder your agent doesn't return your calls! Your reps do not care about your mortgage, or your daughter's braces, or the fact your wife will leave you if you don't find work. They have a job to do and they can only do it when you are helping them — so why aren't you?

Mumbling, murmuring, and complaining are, after all, what keeps us in the desert, waiting to be brought in for a happy landing. Part of the test of being in the wilderness is feeling stuck, but not giving in to *being* stuck. It can all change on a dime with the right attitude — and your attitude is one thing you can control!

So do it.

And when things are going well, say thanks! One of the most delightful things I ever did for my agent, Hilary Wayne, was to buy her a Rolex in honor of our first sale. She loved that thing! She showed everyone whenever we were out together, and it's one of my happiest memories of our relationship. I got to say: Thank you.

So when you feel you must call and complain, when you can't take it anymore, be productive instead: Write something.

CAREERS OUTSIDE THE 310

For those of you who don't live in Los Angeles, don't despair. These days, your career can be handled by using the Internet, mail, plane, and phone. In fact, you might actually do more work, and be less tempted to call, if you aren't down the street from your reps but across the country, or in another one, writing.

I have met many writers in my travels, working pros who've sold specs, done rewrites, and been very successful without ever leaving their hometown. One woman I met in Chicago began writing specs, and selling them, from the confines of her condominium. She did it all by email.

Another great success story is my Screenplayers.org buddy, Jamie Nash, who, from his hometown of Baltimore, has built a career as a writer of quirky sci-fi films like *Altered* (Rogue Pictures) and other assignments, as well as writing and directing his own short films. Jamie is another remarkable go-getter.

It still begs the question: How?

Well, it's the same. Write lots of specs. Get good at your job. Select a few contests — I recommend only a few — and get some feedback. Query groups like Triggerstreet and ScriptShark for better advice. Take a class online. Join a writer's group.

As you get better, pick a project you feel strongest about, get out your *Hollywood Creative Directory*, send out 100 emails, and see what you get back. (If you don't know what an email query is, re-read Chapter One. See! Your skills have been improving just by buying this book.) Attend pitchfests — but don't go expecting to sell something, go to make contacts, get practice at pitching, and keep building up both your skills and your list of professional associates.

And keep doing the following:

▸ Commit to adding to your list of contacts every year.

▸ Keep coming up with high-concept ideas, vet them, write them, rewrite them, put them "on their feet" with a reading.

▸ And continue the process. Write. Sell. Repeat.

At some point, however, you will need to come out here to get the lay of the land. Anyone can plan a two or three-day trip to L.A., and you should. Try to set up meetings with those who have responded to your scripts or pitches, gang up as many as you can, and do them all. Everybody needs practice tear-assing across Laurel Canyon to get from a meeting in Beverly Hills to a busy producer in Burbank.

Why should you be the only one who hasn't?

And when you go back home, make notes of your meetings. No, you don't have to advertise the fact that you live out of town, as long as you are available, and can afford the plane trips between drafts of a script — plus the several emergency trips required to meet, just in case. You can get rewrite jobs, too.

Point is: If you are in the wilderness and want to get out, you have to take the steps. Don't wander in the desert, grumbling about your sad state. Do something. You have to do the work and be prepared to show up for your career with a positive attitude and a love of this adventure. And have no doubt: It is one.

Even when things are going badly.

Even when trouble comes at you in all new ways.

chapter 7

STRIKE BACK U.

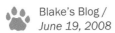 Blake's Blog /
June 19, 2008

"Failure is not an option for us. We are here to succeed. We are here to get closer to our goals by becoming better in the face of a 'no.' And that alone is a 'yes' I can proudly claim every hour of every day!"

Throughout our adventure, from the first *Cat!* book til now, I hope you've been encouraged by one truism that really is true:

There's always a solution.

I learned this as a youth by working with *my* aged screenwriting mentor, Mike Cheda, who calmly, and wisely, held to this notion. I was always in a hurry, impatient, forever forcing the binary: It worked or it didn't, now or never, black or white...

While Mike always clung to "maybe," not enough information yet, and the certainty I hope this book resonates with: Given enough patience to find it, every story problem has an answer.

But is this also true of life?

We've bumped our noses against story trouble, the notes of others — some that we hate — and the challenge of finding and keeping sales reps that not only get our ideas, but get us, too.

We've seen, I hope, that hitting the wall is just the beginning; it's really where the fun starts and the true skill of writing kicks into gear. And I think I've proven the case that if you look at all writing dilemmas this way... you can't fail.

Now I'd like to go further out on a limb and say that these very same rules apply to navigating your way past the Scylla and Charybdi of Hollywood — the Greek myth equivalent of "da shit." One of the nice things about my experience in Movie World is I can share about hitting the wall at absolutely every stage of the profession. From breaking in, to the many ways to screw up along the way, the "dark night of the career" can be beaten, too.

It's how I earned my Masters degree from Strike Back U.

Strike Back University is the school of hard cheese here in Hollywood from which you don't get points for the quality of your work, or selling that big spec, but by rising up from the deck after you've been smacked down hard, and still manage to stand up smiling, ready to go at 'em again. My very first instructor in this discipline was my Dad. His motto, whispered in my ear to the point of annoyance, was: "A Snyder never gives up!" And as an Emmy® award-winning TV producer, he knew whereof he spoke.

He ingrained in me the will to get off the mat and come back swinging. A pioneer in children's television, my father walked an even scarier high-wire act than I ever have. Often it was only after the fact, when the show had been bought, or the first check was finally received, that he'd let the wife and kids know he'd had to mortgage the house as a stake against his latest venture.

His incredible career, filled with million-dollar paychecks and Peabody Awards, was a testament to the *real* family motto:

Whew!

We screenwriters have a much lower overhead. It's just the cost of paper, brads, and the patience of our loved ones. But the lessons we can derive from sampling the courses taught at Strike Back U. are still required.

So what do we offer here at Ol' Cat?

BREAKING IN 101

Whenever my former writing partner, Sheldon Bull, was asked how he broke into the business, Sheldon's response was: "Late at night." And there is still some truth to that. Strike Back U. welcomes freshmen. To be admitted to this most basic of first-term survey courses, we encourage you to write a lot of spec screenplays, learn about the business by studying trade journals such as *Variety* and *The Hollywood Reporter*, and sampling a summer reading list that includes *What Makes Sammy Run?*; *Hello, He Lied*; *Breakfast With Sharks*; and *Adventures in the Screen Trade*. Once admitted, you'll face tests that seem to have little to do with writing, but everything to do with career.

Nothing is more indicative of your freshman status, and a trait we strive to correct, than being over-eager. You've got the stuff, we know that, and yet there are right and wrong ways to introduce yourself... and transcend the mistakes we all make:

▸ *Overly familiar too fast* — You meet someone at a party, event, or even the supermarket. They're a "name" and your follow-up is a barrage of calls and emails or dropping by the office unannounced that makes them wish they'd never met you. You've taken a nice interaction and become a stalker. You've been gifted by chance to know someone better, and leaped ahead, bragging to all who'll listen about your new best friend. Well, don't. This is great if you're David Geffen, if you're a *wunderkind* in the making who is kicking butt and taking names, but freshmen who over-commit too fast only reveal a lack of long-term planning.

▸ *Pushing for the meeting, and blowing it* — The amazing fact for freshman is you *can* get a meeting with a bigwig. Surprise! In fact, as a new face in town you actually have more sizzle than many veterans. You are an unknown quantity, in a community forever craving fresh ideas, and — especially if you are young — are assumed to have knowledge of the target market execs pretend to know, but don't. So if you push for a meeting, they might meet you. But if you get the face time, use it wisely, and make it count. Because if you get in that room and you don't dazzle, it will be a while — and you'll have to do something remarkable — to be invited back.

▸ *Confusing "no" for "yes"* — There are a million ways for a producer to pass on a project, e.g., "I like the idea, but not the script"; "It needs a little more set-up"; "I'm going to Cannes and when I come back we'll talk about it." These are all… "no." The producer's job is to let you down easy — and yet sometimes we don't get it. Often freshman confuse these non-denial denials as "maybe." We've seen frosh throw themselves at these little shafts of daylight hoping to push open the door, by rewriting based on a note that's really a "no," and spending weeks and months to little avail. Yes is "yes." Yes is: "Call business affairs!" Everything else is "no." Proceed at your own risk — and on your own dime.

Another maddening thing about freshman year that BREAK- ING IN 101 helps to overcome is the problem of not being a member and only being allowed to become a member if you already are one.

Huh?

Hollywood is rife with Catch 22's. "Have your agent send the script, otherwise we can't read it," you'll hear. But you don't have an agent and when you contact one, they'll say: "I can't take you on unless you have a deal." *Grrrr*. Another example of this kind of doubletalk is: As a freshman, you'll desperately want to join the Writers Guild of America (*www.wga.com*). There is a point system whereby so many credits earned gets you in. Yet you will often be precluded from getting jobs because you aren't in the WGA. But if you can't get jobs to earn the points… *Grrrr 2*.

And still we all survive and even go on to prosper.

How?

The way past all these roadblocks, and what BREAKING IN 101 stresses, is the development of — and momentum for — your real talent and skills. Take a breath. Take it easy. And know that there is nothing that will get you in the door faster, and keep you there, than steady improvement in your writing chops and a slowly earned reputation for quality work and great ideas.

Yes, there are frustrations:

▸ The reader working for an agency, company, or studio who seems to have it in for you. Often, he is just like you, a writer on the make, sandbagging others.

▸ A buyer who dangles $100,000 for a script, but can't commit, so you think cutting your price will help. How about $50,000? $25,000? You'll take it! But what this buyer is really saying is… "no." Fooled ya! This game was over the minute you caved.

▸ The agent who charges reading fees, or has some odd scheme for representing you, or is interested in your script only because it is like his "real" client's and he wants to see if yours is competition.

All these and more will perplex you, and make you think it's about you. And make you do something crazy — like quit.

Don't.

Keep firing with scripts they can't say "no" to, keep up the attack with concepts, pitches, and treatments that wow. Keep building your sheaf of contacts — the right way — by putting yourself in their shoes and asking: If I were them, why would I want to be in business with me? And then deliver on that insight.

And remember my father, SBU professor emeritus' advice, which should sustain us through the perils of freshman-itis:

Every "no" is one step closer to a "yes."

HEAT AND YOU: AN OVERVIEW

A slightly advanced course offered all who attend Strike Back U. is more upbeat. There will come a time when you actually sell something. In fact, you might have your name in the trades, and an article listing your latest achievements appearing on the front page of both *Variety* and *The Hollywood Reporter*. Amazing! Like Will Ferrell in *Anchorman*, you will find yourself saying: "I don't know how to put this... but I'm kind of a big deal."

Congratulations. You have "heat."

We might go so far as to call you "hot."

And while so many screenwriting schools focus on the can'ts, that's how Strike Back U. is different.

Because we know you can.

Your rise in temperature is due to many factors. You may have sold a spec, written a troubled film into production, or hatched a pitch that's packaged with an "in" star, but the point is you have everything you've needed to move to the next level.

So what is that?

HEAT AND YOU: AN OVERVIEW teaches students how to parlay their thermal inversion and not misuse it. Oddly, becoming known puts you in a place where there is risk. Believe it or not, this is just one more test. You can take your heat and parlay it *down* the ladder as easily as you can go the other way. The classic cautionary tale is best seen in the documentary, *Overnight* (2003), in which said writer, by his own admission, did just this.

The proper use of warmth veering on heat is to go back to a basic question we should be asking at all points in our lives:

> *If a magic wand was waved over me right now,*
> *and I could have anything I wanted, what would that be?*

In truth, you should be prepared with a response at every stage of your career, because the answer will keep changing.

Early on, your one and only dream is to "sell something," to "get on the boards," but now that you have that, what next? You certainly want to get a great movie made, stay on the project as long as possible, make the final product as good as what's in your imagination. But more often you are fired or rewritten. Sadly, the writer is thought disposable here, Hollywood being the only relay race where you hand the baton to the next guy...

And he shoots you.

So regardless of the outcome, you decide to live up to the motto of our curriculum, and our graduates, and... strike back!

Suddenly the wish you'd make if you had a magic wand (that worked) is to ingratiate yourself into your deal as either a director or a producer. Consulting with your reps, and with the next script being as hot as the first one you sold, you can.

The list is long of writers who, by original design or out of necessity to protect their work and stay in the game, made being a producer or a director a key to their next sale.

And if you don't like this avenue, you might consider partnering up with someone who has a producer or director head, but is lacking writer skills. Andrew Bergman and his producing partner Mike Lobell for many years structured their deals thusly, Bergman parlaying his writer's heat properly — demanding not a full bar, or a ride in a G-5, or front row seats at the premiere, or a date with a pretty actress (we've heard of writers using their heat for even more inconsequential stuff), but a greater role in making and controlling projects that had his personal voice. The result is a long list of successful films as both writer and director (among them: *The Freshman*, *Honeymoon in Vegas*, *It Could Happen to You*), delivered in Bergman's unique style and protected by producing partner Lobell from the nabobs who could easily have taken his baton, turned, and shot him... then run the other way.

When it comes to directing, it all sounds very fun, but here's a hint: Don't insist you want to direct... *just cuz*.

If you *must* write-and-direct that's one thing, but if you want to be the name above the title because your friend did it, or because it's cool, or because Quentin Tarantino does... don't.

Here's the way to know if directing is for you:

1. You have a burning desire to do it

2. You love incredibly hard work

Having heat also allows you access to others with heat. Out of the blue, you will find yourself in rooms with people you have admired from afar for years who are suddenly telling you:

"Let's work on something together!"

Yes, Jeffrey! You bet, George! No doubt about it, Wendy! We absolutely *should* do something together a-s-freakin'-a-p.

It's not farfetched to be hatching these plans and these scenarios early. Instead of picking up the phone and calling your agent when you're bored and moody and think you're not going anywhere, why not sketch out a few "dream plans" where it's just you and ___ hanging out (it could happen) and "working together" comes up.

This is what HEAT AND YOU: AN OVERVIEW teaches: Think ahead, dream big dreams, and review these plans every year.

We ask that you work out with breathtaking audacity:

- ▸ A one-year plan
- ▸ A five-year plan
- ▸ A ten-year plan

And be specific.

What other writer's career most resembles the one you want?

What steps did that writer take to achieve his or her goals?

These scenarios, I can tell you, when written down (or better yet spoken aloud) have amazing power to actually occur.

Be ready.

CRITICAL MELTDOWN: A BRIEF HISTORY

To take this class there are pre-requisites; you have to write and sell a script, and get your name on the credits of the movie when it's widely released. That is the requirement for being in the crosshairs of America's most beloved pastime:

Bashing Hollywood!

The flipside of having heat, and just as treacherous, is to have a script with your name on it get made and be lambasted mercilessly by critics. Yet many of our finest graduates have experienced this very problem and not only survived, but thrived.

Fricasseeing the latest movie that comes out of Hollywood is not only okay, it's good sport in America. It's so easy to pan a "commercial" film. And the ones that are merely entertaining are criticized most. Movies are as easily available as water, so we just expect more to come out of the tap. Look at what Siskel and Ebert popularized to deal with the horn 'o plenty pouring out of the 310 area code: Thumbs up or thumbs down. That's it! Just like Roman emperors voting on the life or death of the poor gladiator, bleeding in the arena, who only wanted to put on a good show.

Did these fine critics sit with the writer in his kitchen, watching his bills mount up, wives or girlfriends crying, begging him to stop! And yet he persevered! Did A.O. Scott read *all* the drafts the script went through to see how an anonymous studio executive and his anonymous writer took a left turn on draft #20, sending the script down the road to a green light, sure, but away from a document that actually started out written... *in English*.

And now... *isn't*?

And when the bashing is doled out, it's always the script! That poor director, those poor actors! Look at the trash they had to work with! These are the people the critic will meet in Cannes. The poor writer is back home with his Fruit Loops, thinking about a new idea that maybe, just maybe, might be critic proof.

The reason this course is necessary, and one you must be aware of, is: You too will experience this scorching. Your script will be bought, and then one day you'll pick up the trades and read that it's getting made. You're the last person to know, of course. They stopped calling you to tell you about the progress of your story months ago. And then it is made and released, and the cry of "bomb" and "disaster" and "stinker" suddenly is about you, yet you're the person who had the least to do with how it turned out.

You may again want to quit, you may take it personally when you read the reviews and take the criticism to heart. But look at the list of writers whose first movies were horrible disasters. What if these talented writers said: "You're right. I suck." and quit:

Phil Alden Robinson's first movie was *Rhinestone*...
... but he went on to write *Field of Dreams*.

Bob Zemeckis' first few films underwhelmed until...
... he and Bob Gale wrote *Back to the Future*.

Scott Alexander & Larry Karaszewski's *Problem Child*...
... led them to *The People vs. Larry Flynt*.

The awful truth? Hollywood cares very little about critics, because critics have very little to say about whether or not a movie is a hit. And here's another terrible secret: Critics are often wrong. A short list of movies bashed by critics include:

It's a Wonderful Life
Bonnie and Clyde
Willy Wonka & The Chocolate Factory (1971)
Blade Runner

Point is: You will have a movie made one day. And given the nature of current critical etiquette — especially for any movie considered simply "entertaining" or "genre" or "just for fun" — you too will be scorched by critics. Most recently, the movie *Four Christmases* faced this dilemma. This was cited in the first *Cat!* book as a great example of a concept that worked; it went on to attract top talent including Vince Vaughn, Reese Witherspoon, Robert Duvall, and Sissy Spacek; opened #1, sustained #1 status for three weeks, and grossed over $120,000,000 in the U.S. alone.

It got a 22% favorable rating on Rotten Tomatoes.

Lighting their cigars at Warner Brothers, the executives who greenlit this movie are literally laughing all the way to the bank, and *Four Christmases* will be a holiday perennial that will do just as well or better in its DVD release. Rotten *who*?

Strike Back U. teaches us to have a thick skin. If you are so lucky to join the exclusive club of writers who've had a movie made (an odds-defying feat in itself), you will soon realize how everyone who isn't in... wishes they were. You entertain millions of people, and uplift and enlighten with your work. Don't let any critic kill your spirit. Don't empower ignorance and jealousy.

No criticism can stop you from achieving your goals...
and no critic knows the whole story.

INTRODUCTION TO PARTNERS

There is no "I" in team, and writing partnerships prove it.

The pros and cons of being a pair — or trio — are spelled out in this elective detailing one of the most rewarding relationships in the film business.

On the plus side, a partner — or partners — takes half or more of the workload off your shoulders. He or she is right there with you in meetings, someone to complain to when business is bad, and your best bud to celebrate with when the going is good.

On the downside, you are partners, which means you split all monies and residual payments (the difference between "and" and "&" on any writing credit can mean millions of dollars). And if you disagree, or if you suddenly can't stand to look at this person, you're stuck.

Rules for finding and maintaining partnerships include:

▸ Aim high. Find someone who is a better writer than you are, or has skills you don't have. If you're a whiz at structure, work with the person who's great with character or dialogue.

▸ Have similar goals. It's a terrible surprise to learn your partner harbors a secret urge to direct and has been using this relationship to further that desire, so find out early.

▸ No quibbling. Lame is the partnership where progress is stalled because one of you stands on a line, nuance, character, or scene. Discuss, yes. Argue, sure. Shout, of course. But settle it. And move on.

In the day-to-day operation of your partnership it's good to have office hours, set times where you go to work, have lunch, and agree to stop. The best partnerships aren't personal; rare is the team that also socializes after hours. We are friendly, not familiar.

And when it comes to techniques for actually writing:

▶ Over the shoulder. Literally you work in the same room, taking turns as each of you takes a whack at the scene, writing over the other, one after the next, reading aloud till satisfied.

▶ Draft swap. You take the first pass, write it all the way into rough draft, and hand it off to your partner. He takes the next whack at it, until you are ready to polish together.

▶ Long Distance. Technology allows partners to write together and not be in the same room. There is even software (Zhura) that facilitates you both being able to see the page as you take turns writing, while you talk (or don't) via the usual means.

The best meeting etiquette is to remember there *is* no "I" in team. The most successful partnerships think "we" not "I," and the best ones soon forget who wrote what — and really don't care. You must respect your partner, and vice versa. And like any good relationship, you will get sick of each other at times — but mostly you both enjoy the process.

Breaking up is hard to do. And one of the downsides of partnership is *not* knowing who did what. Now each of you has an agent, and a stack of scripts with both your names on them, that neither writer can fairly use as samples of his work. Some great partnerships that went south include the husband and wife team of Nancy Meyers and Charles Shyer, with each going on to individual success, but with the community wondering, really, who was doing what all along? And some of the greatest partnerships, such as Billy Wilder — who worked with I.A.L. Diamond, Raymond Chandler, and Charles Brackett — were about a director working with a writer to create something for him to direct and produce. The Coen brothers and the Wachowskis each work this way.

Unique variations on the writing partnership have been attempted by super talents such as Ron Bass (*Rain Man, My Best Friend's Wedding*), who hires a team of writers and has them under contract in a kind of atelier. It's much like a Renaissance painter who might run a studio that bears his brand but to which multiple apprentices contribute.

There is always a new way to work together. At Strike Back U. we encourage all such collaborations. Not only is there safety in numbers, but a solid partnership can turn out great work fast, and with the least amount of writer whining.

The best teams are 1 + 1 = 3. You are better together than you are apart. Each owes everything to his or her better half, who sat with you while you went through your divorce, put up with your annoying o.c.d. habit of always making sure the page breaks look nice, and let you down easy when the joke you try dies a miserable death. There's nothing better than true partnership, and the best ones pay tribute to this unique bond. Yes it's true:

There's no "I" in team...
... but in a good *team there is plenty of I. O. U.*

AGENT SWITCH

As stated earlier, agents tell writers they will spend the first half of your career putting you into a box and the second half getting you out of it. Hence this elective, for what happens when the box the agent put you in is a coffin... and the agent is hammering the nails?

If you are uncertain if your agent's time on Planet You is growing short, try taking this simple, if teasing, pop quiz:

1. When my agent calls and tells me I have a meeting with "one of the Wilsons," I assume he means...

    a. Owen

    b. Luke

    c. Mr.

2. The last time my agent called, it was to inform me...
   a. I had just sold a big project to the studio
   b. I had just received an offer from a top producer
   c. I owed the agency money for postage

3. My agent represents me because of...
   a. My years of experience
   b. My multi-faceted talent
   c. My incriminating photos from the Disney retreat

If you answered (c.) to any of the above, it may be time to switch agents. Your rep has lost interest, or doesn't know how to sell you. It's painful but true: It's time to commit *tenpercenticide*.

But how do you handle the time honored "agent switch" — and still keep your integrity intact?

We hate sneakiness at Strike Back U. Our motto, translated from the Latin, is "ethics, ethics, ethics" because we know that when the points are totaled, it is better to have played the game honorably.

And yet...

If you really have decided to switch agents, you have to play this horrible game... without telling your agent you're doing it. Like looking for a job while remaining at the one you're in, you become less attractive if you have no home.

So you must keep your foot on base till you're ready to go.

Odds are if you are on the market for new representation, part of the problem is your lack of heat. You have to do something that will raise your temperature without your agent, so that you can bring yourself and your new ideas to someone else.

This means letting it be known you are "in play." And this is where having a lawyer or a manager who is also aware of these problems can really help. Maybe you're just overly sensitive? Maybe you just have task avoidance about the latest assignment your agent got you that you're stuck on? It's usually best to get someone else's opinion about your situation because you are not always the best judge. And if you think stirring things up will generate new heat, the word quietly gets out.

"In play" means that if anyone out there is interested in representing you, they may now consider it fair game to take you to lunch to talk about your career — not that this hasn't stopped them from doing so before. Only you had kyboshed that before. We hope.

Nothing is worse than an agent flirt.

If you are serious about switching agents, great. But don't schedule a meeting with one and be coy about it. If you want new representation, fine; if you just want lunch, buy it yourself.

And get ready for action. The pitch from possible new agents will be overwhelming.

All kinds of new techniques for representation will be laid at your feet, for example (drum roll), the agent "team"! Someone to represent you in TV, in new media, *and* with corporate America (meaning you can write commercials on the side). Mostly what the new agency will be stressing, without being petty, is how your current agent does not appreciate you, and how they do, and will serve you better.

Will they?

What you are looking for is not the dazzling wheels and gears of the new agency, but the who. Are you sensing that the new guy or gal across from your Chinese Chicken Salad gets you? Is there a burning desire in your heart that is not being met, a lack of attention to, or staleness in your current relationship that will be revitalized or enhanced with this new person?

It's a gut reaction.

Return to your earlier course work in HEAT AND YOU: AN OVERVIEW. Review your one-, five-, and ten-year plans and see how they are being met by your current agent. But remember, the new agent really, bottom line, doesn't have any more contacts or insights than your last agent, only different ones. And remember too, as far along as you are in your career, nothing's changed:

Whaddya got for me?

The Big Picture: "Get me Beach Nuts!" One of the best cautionary tales about Hollywood ever, *The Big Picture* captures lunch with an agent (Martin Short as Neil Sussman) that still rings true.

Maybe before any of this dance with a new agent begins, you should come up with something like a new spec screenplay, a virgin no one's seen that you'd be willing to show a new agent if she says the right things. But be careful, too. Agency **coverage** is forever. When you hand a script to any agent, you must assume it will be turned over to agency readers, reviewed, and catalogued for better or worse, and even be made available to studios. Ideas we can share forever, but actual scripts — especially virgin specs — are gold, and their value decreases the moment you hand one off to anyone.

You also want to know: Who are your contacts? Who can you get me to that my current agent can't? Only you can say how important this is, based on your present and future goals.

At the end of the day, you can call up your new suitor, or let it be known through the person who set up the meeting, that it's either a go or not. Strike Back U. recommends that you always be open to finding those people who can help sell you best. But switching agents is like plastic surgery: Don't get addicted. An agent face lift will only help revitalize you so much, but if you start switching as a matter of course, your lips shot up with Botox and your eyes lifted with every new makeover, you can look like what you've become: used goods. Avoid this. Switching agents, like getting an agent, only takes you so far. The real work is the writing skill you must forever be improving.

A new agent can help revive your career...
... but doesn't make a new you.

ANTI-AGING AND WRITER REJUVENATION

Is there ageism in Hollywood?

Yes and no.

We can cite hundreds of writers who feel there is, and can claim it was "being over 40" that did them in (not realizing it was the fact their ideas were "over 40"). For every sad story there is a hopeful one. Alvin Sargent, a Strike Back U. All-Star, had been writing for 40 years when he hit *Spider-Man 2* out of the ballpark. And Horton Foote was going strong well into his 90s. In TV, it may be true, but in movies, we care less about someone's age and more about their ability to write primal, meaningful stories. For those breaking in late, this seems like a barrier.

It's not.

And yet like considering getting a new agent, the phrase "re-inventing yourself" comes up after a certain point. If you've reached a dead end, or feel like you have, what can you do to jump-start your sagging career, and make yourself appear trimmer?

▸ Youth injection. We know many an older writer who has paired up with a younger one. There is merit to this tactic. It's in a sense a fair swap: my experience for your fresh approach and insight into a market I may no longer understand.

▸ Working for free. This doesn't mean giving away work; it means working on projects like short films, webcasts, etc., that aren't paying gigs, but may lead to them. If you don't need the money and like to experiment, it might be the best way to pursue your more creative, less commercial, side, too.

▸ The Other Side of the Desk. Many writers moonlight in development, often taking jobs that help them get a better feel for the market, so that when they write their projects on the side, they have a better chance of selling. Many times you will see development executives put a pseudonym on their spec script when it's sent out, not only to avoid conflict of interest if it sells, but embarrassment if it does not. Overall, this is a great way to keep in the game.

These strategies for rebooting your career can work, as do attempts to play producer. Many times the screenwriter will graduate to a producer role, parlaying early success as a writer and then buying the rights to a news story, novel, or other property — and attaching himself not as writer, but as producer. See, there are all kinds of ways to skin Ol' Cat, and being fleet of foot, sensitive like a Cat! burglar to every noise in the night, and forever attuned to the changing winds is the only way to be.

And that's what Strike Back U. is about:

It's not personal, it's business…
… and there's plenty for everybody!

STRIKE BACK U. SABBATICALS: LEAVING LOS ANGELES

Sometimes when all else fails, we have to pick up our ball and jacks and go elsewhere. Whether long term or short term, getting out of Dodge can be a healthy reboot for writers who find themselves stalled in L.A. at any stage of their careers. Be advised it's not the only game… or the only town.

We spend our careers trying to break into the business, then one day the smart move appears to be breaking out. And one of the solutions many screenwriters are finding is moving away from Hollywood to "film towns" that offer a new freedom and a revitalized sense of the possibilities the business has always offered. Hollywood, remember, was in itself an escape destination. It was running from Thomas Edison and East Coast film syndicates impairing their ability to be free that led pioneers to settle in Hollywood and begin the Golden Era in the first place.

There is an argument the era is over and that the business is going the way of the music industry, with more independents, do-it-yourselfers, and wildcat entrepreneurs who need only a narrow but loyal audience to continue making a living. Perhaps, the current wisdom goes, those seeking more freedom should take their act out of town — often for good.

And there is quite a variety of locations to choose from.

In my travels I have discovered many such spots, some for real, some yet to emerge, and a few not as advertised. These cities offer the most hope for Hollywood II:

Austin, Texas — "It's like *Mommie, Dearest* and you're the kid who only knows what it's like to be beaten, and then one day you have a new mother. It's like a brand new life." This is the description writer Anton Diether used to recommend his decision to move from L.A. after a 20-year career. After years of being rewritten and told "you're the writer, just write," Anton is now pursuing both writing and producing, and Austin has proved the perfect spot. As a film community, the city has great prospects for becoming the real deal. Both the annual Austin Film Festival and South by Southwest offer access to Austin's other great creative community, the music business, and the talent pool for both above and below the line is indicative of a bright future. Directors Robert Rodriguez and Richard Linklater, and stars like Sandra Bullock and Matthew McConaughey call it home. The true test of a film town is talent, not just tax breaks or "facilities," and Austin has not only the creative chops but an independent streak a mile wide... and bats!

Atlanta, Georgia — All planes go through Atlanta, an air travel hub. The city's always been a busy commercial center for advertising and industrial film, and has a vibrant music industry too. Tyler Perry has made camp here, operating a booming studio that does both TV series and films. Perry also has one of the best methods for evaluating films to be produced: the church play circuit. Weekends find Perry testing out his stories, much like stage performers in years past tried out material for their movies on the nightclub circuit. His studio is the center of a definite revival in independent filmmaking here, and though plagued by initial conflicts with both the WGA and the DGA, the balance of being away from L.A. has worked for Perry and others in this growing film community.

Vancouver, British Columbia — The tax breaks are still great in Canada and the film business thrives here (and in Toronto). Like raising money to make movies anywhere, there is red tape involved, but here it's the governmental kind. Those bureaucrats play favorites just like at the studios. Lots of series production, especially American cable fare, is located here. Many B.C. professionals have lives in both L.A. and Vancouver.

Portland, Oregon/Seattle, Washington — Kind of a tie between these two places. Portland's film scene is wildly independent, with local patron saint Gus Van Sant the leading light in the city's Pearl District, and a great annual film festival. Seattle, on the other hand, has a vibrant indie biz too, with lots of writers groups like the Northwest Screenwriters, and lots of contests, short film festivals, and independent theaters and actors ready to work. Both cities are populated with L.A. escapees, many of whom use the relatively short commute to justify living in the Northwest but still working in Hollywood.

Other cities and countries around the world offer similar chances for escape. UK, Australia, South Africa, India, Hong Kong, China, and Brazil have a growing global presence and an appetite for seasoned Hollywood filmmakers looking for a change of pace. Yes, there always is a new film community springing up somewhere, but the goal remains the same. Leaving Los Angeles is a great way to use what you have gathered here at Strike Back U. and take it to a place where these lessons can be put to use.

TUITION

The best news about Strike Back U. is: Tuition is free. Whether you take classes in Los Angeles, New York, Chicago, London, or Sydney, or in the farflung campuses of India, Hong Kong, South Africa, and Eastern Europe, the rigors are similar, and both challenging and exciting. You the writer have a free pass to jump in and start learning.

And it's better than film school.

Putting yourself into the work-a-day world, trying to beat the system that is both welcoming and guarded at the same time, is the real test. And keeping your wits about you is really a matter of knowing what you want — and what you can deliver.

But the final subject, which we'll talk about next, is not taught in any school.

chapter 8

 Blake's Last Blog /
August 3, 2009

"The most important
thing to do is to
love what you're
doing. That way,
getting better at it
isn't a struggle, it's
a pleasure."

DISCIPLINE, FOCUS, AND POSITIVE ENERGY

At the outset of this book, I boldly declared that I was about to offer you a soup-to-nuts guide for how to get out of any frustrating corner writers find ourselves stuck in.

But have we missed the odd bisque, or random filbert?

We've talked about all manner of story problems, from concept and logline to the hurdle of presenting both.

We've examined the fine points of every section of a script and seen how each has its own demand and tone.

We've gone over the mental body English (is there such a term?) required to sit still while executives who've paid us to write, rip apart our beautiful writage.

And we've given you some really lovely "inside the Beltway" tips on how to find, keep, and *hondle* your career — discussing everything from firing an agent, to finding a writing partner, to coming to grips with the possibility your future is *outside* the Beltway.

So what are we missing?

Ah, yes! My favorite!

The subject we haven't discussed, not overtly anyway, is that part of the process that is invisible — that part of "hitting the wall" that, like the hero of every good story, requires you to "dig, deep down" and find the inner strength that goes beyond the material world, that part of tapping into the big picture in which you too are touched by something you've heard of, but maybe don't believe in.

Yet.

And if I am a man of my word, and I am, I will now attempt to discuss this powerful experience.

But only if you promise not to tell.

This is just you and me talking now.

That screenwriter who won an Oscar® with his very first screenplay, we'll say a quiet prayer for him. We who have to struggle to find our stride, we who bang our noggins against the wall not getting it, I'm letting you know right now, are ahead of the game when it comes to this part. Because if you are six scripts in and haven't sold a thing, if you are stuck on a script you know is "the one" but can't get it right, if you're sure you have "the stuff" and yet are not quite connecting, all the tools — and all the success in the world — won't give you this part.

Are you ready?

WHY DO THEY CALL IT "THE DARK NIGHT OF THE SOUL"?

What your writing career boils down to is: Do you want it?

And if you do: To say so.

It's that simple.

We move through our careers facing any number of obstacles — from people in our lives, to actual (no kidding) rejection. I mentioned Aunt Fern in the Introduction. There is no Aunt Fern, she's just a composite of every relative we will meet at Thanksgiving who does not understand. We love Aunt Fern. She means well. But when she comes up to you and looks you in the eye and says: "How's the writing coming?" that's not what she means. What she means is:

"When are you going to give up this dream of yours and join all us normal people over here by the yams?"

Aunt Fern is an amateur, but professionals take this role too — actual people with actual jobs in the business who will say: "Go home! Quit! You're not good enough!" The odd reader coverage about your script that you get your hands on can curl the hair of the bravest among us. What is the coverage on *you*? That's what it feels like. And many a professional with lots of time to her credit may even try to do you a favor, and let you down easy. "Go back to Kansas. You don't fit in here. You'll never make it."

And why shouldn't we believe them?

Deep down in our own souls, we wonder.

Yet throughout this book, if you've been reading between the lines, there are messages written just to you that tell you that to quit would be an error. To give up now would not only be a shame, but wrong, a giant wooden shoe thrown into the wheelhouse of what should be. And if you are truly meant to pursue this career, to have success in this or any endeavor, these messages are crystal clear, shouting loudly in your ear.

Do you hear them?

If you do, you're on the right track.

If you don't, you might not be.

It's all about finding your place in the world, so wherever you end up, you will be okay if you listen and abide.

Because this is where I found myself, at that very crossroad, wondering what I should do next, and I tried it.

And it changed my life.

1989

Things were bad.

I had been in Hollywood seven years and had little to claim for it. I'd written a couple of TV shows, gotten into the WGA, and had a few things optioned, but was otherwise a failure.

So I went home. It wasn't Kansas; it was Santa Barbara, a mere 90 miles away from Hollywood, and if you like exile, there's no better place for it. But I might as well have been in Kansas.

Seven years in, nobody knew me. And nobody cared.

I'd actually had professionals tell me, or tell others who told me, that I would never make it in this man's business. I had read the coverage on me. But I didn't have to. My plan to work part-time jobs and write on the side was getting me nowhere. And all my best ideas were not connecting with holders of checkbooks.

I was 31.

In January, my father died.

I joke about the All Is Lost point being the place where all mentors go to die. Obie-Wan dies on page 75 in *Star Wars*, if only to allow Luke to go the rest of the way on his own. These story beats resonate for a reason — because they happen in real life, too. The feeling of being left on your own early, having not yet fulfilled the mission you were assigned, was a very real one for me. So what was I doing wrong and, more importantly, what should I do about it? My very concerned and caring girlfriend suggested getting my teaching credential just to have something to fall back on. But I was resisting. It felt like being a lobster in a pot of slowly boiling water. Get in! The water's fine! I was being told.

If I surrendered one degree at a time, maybe it wouldn't be so bad.

I was a night writer back then. I had a laptop and used to go to the only 24-hour coffee shop in town, The Fig Tree, to at least be a writer in public. And then one late night, looking over the empty tables, watching a clutch of waitresses giggling together, I was right on the brink of giving up. Yams. Got plenty, right here. They're really good for you. Just take a bite.

What transpired next defies rationality.

It came from my Dad.

My Dad was the ultimate optimist. He liked to tell the joke about the little boy who was so sunshiny that his father decided to teach him a lesson one Christmas morning. The father filled the kid's stocking with horse manure, expecting to see his son finally disappointed, only to be amazed when — upon finding this joke gift — the boy ran excitedly around the living room, looking behind every nook and cranny, exclaiming: "There must be a pony!"

That was my Dad. And that was his maxim for life.

But where did he get it from?

Shortly after my father died, I found a box of his favorite books. And as I dug in and starting reading them, I began to see where all his positivism came from and why he thought that way. There were lots of books that explained it. And by reading them, I started to see what I'd been doing wrong — in my career and my life. I had been resisting my father's jolly optimism forever. That upbeat attitude seemed naïve, and worse than that, a denial of "the truth about the world." Yet with him gone, and without getting the chance to ask him anymore, what I was finding was in fact denial of the truth about myself:

▸ I'd been a bullhead — it's true! I was much more interested in doing it my way than succeeding.

▸ I'd been all over the map, writing TV scripts, movies, sketches, even radio. But more than that, I had been thinking small, and mostly thinking about me.

▸ I had not been hearing the people who were trying to help me, ignoring the messages that were loud and clear from all corners.

And all had led to an even greater crime. In a world of glorious possibility — at a time and place where opportunity was all around me — I was standing in a field full of diamonds, refusing to reach down and just pick one up.

Even though my Dad was gone, I heard him more than I ever had before. And maybe because he was gone, everything he had taught me that I had ignored, every heroic act I had seen him perform — including the brave optimism he had shown in the way he died — now seemed to be what the real lesson of his life had been. All the goofy slogans and the "glass half full" outlook that never waned was the real theme of his life. He could've been anyone, and done anything, but the message would always be the same:

Believe in yourself and never quit.

THE TURN

There is a cosmic law that lets us know almost immediately that we are on the right track. Up until the point when you have a "moment of clarity," it really doesn't seem possible to change. And then when you do, the floodgates open. Yet all it ever really takes is a decision — and just the tiniest action step as proof.

What was mine? What amazing action changed it all?

I bought an orange, College ruled, Note-Tote notebook.

It was to be my diary — and I still have it, along with all the others that have followed. And here was my first entry:

"How To Be A Famous Screenwriter — April 22, 1989 — This is to be my daily diary of how I became a famous screenwriter. It is to encompass notes on movies I see, ideas, sketches, and movie plots. It will also include my own strategies including how they worked, or didn't, and why. Mostly it is a step-by-step account of how I ultimately succeeded in writing for the movies."

Can you imagine the audacity of this?

I shared this story with — and read this entry to — my audience at Screenwriting Expo in 2008 and was embarrassed to say it out loud. Here was a guy who was, by every conceivable standard, so far away from making this claim that it bordered on delusion. I had no agent. I had no prospects. And did I mention I was broke? Oh man. This was the period when I had to dig coins out of the couch to treat myself to a cup of coffee along State Street. And yet with that simple action, everything started to change.

I had decided to change. I'd decided to win.

Synthesizing all the aphorisms and techniques I had been reading about into *my* way — we bullheads die hard — I took a look at the following laundry list of my deficits, determined to kill these old ideas about myself and create new ideas and new truths:

▸ I lacked discipline. My very mopiness about my situation meant that on some days I didn't write because I wasn't in the mood. I rationalized this, of course, and didn't notice that often I'd not written for weeks. But if I was to be "Open for Business" here in the universe then I had to keep business hours.

▸ I lacked focus. I had been dabbling. And by seeing it suddenly not just from my perspective, but from someone who might be eager to buy something from me, I realized: How could they? What was I? What specialty did I offer? What was my service? I was impossible to find, or even see, because I had no silhouette. When they thought of me the writer, what did they think? Well, nothing. I'd thrown myself in all directions, not mastering one.

▸ I also lacked my father's positivity. If someone gave me a stocking full of horse manure, I'd cry. The idea of turning nothing into something just by seeing it from another angle made my brain hurt. And yet there were examples in my Dad's life, and many in the books I'd read, of that very thing. Could the power of perspective, the power of one's mind, turn gossamer into gold? Could the right mental leverage on a situation somehow change it?

Again, I did something small.

Knowing what I knew, I took another gi-normous action step:

I bought index cards.

On the first index card I wrote my wild goals — proclaimed in the affirmative tense as though they were real. I made sure they were as crazy out there, as pie in the sky as they could be:

> ▶ *I have sold a script for a million dollars*
> ▶ *I have a multi-picture deal with a major studio*
> ▶ *I have an office on the lot*

Again, I can't stress how insane this was.

And just to make sure I would keep reminding myself how to stay on track, I took a second index card and wrote this:

> ▶ *Discipline*
> ▶ *Focus*
> ▶ *Positive Energy*

And that's when the flood began.

Like I say, it's a law. And it's simple. By declaring that I had been changed, I was. By setting goals and sticking to them, they started to appear. And in a very short order proof came.

Out of the blue, my pal Tommy Lynch called and hired me to write more television shows for him. It wasn't much, but it was enough to let me write full time, and gave me a great excuse to go to L.A. and the set where my episodes were being taped. Walking downtown in Santa Barbara one day, my girlfriend saw an office for rent above a bar, cheap enough for me to afford. Suddenly I was no longer a night writer but one with office hours… and a place to hang my index cards.

DISCIPLINE, FOCUS, AND POSITIVE ENERGY

When I think of the snapshot of my happiest time, it was that summer. Broke, yes. Scared, sure. But every day, things kept getting better, and more people started to appear, as if by magic, to assist me in achieving my secret wishes. Looking back on it now, everything that happened bears a startling resemblance to "Storming the Castle." Doesn't it? That's why these things ring so true in stories — because they are true.

It began with a proactive decision, a "turn into Three" in which I set a goal, gathered tools, made amends to my allies, and set about to pass the "Final Exam" and "rescue the Princess."

And everything was driven by that phrase, one I kept repeating like a mantra during all the in-between moments:

Discipline, Focus, and Positive Energy.

It guided everything I did.

How was I disciplined? I made sure that I did something *every day* to move my career forward. Not only did I write something (even if I threw it away the next day), I made a goal of a number of pages, and a deadline to write them. When I ran out of juice in the afternoon, I wrote letters or made phones calls to possible connections. And lucky for me, my allies now appeared too, primary among them Jim Haggin, who at the ripe old age of 24 had sold a script to Disney, and "got it" more than anyone I knew. Whenever I could, I met with him to pick his brain and bounce off new ideas.

How was I focused? Realizing that I had no specialty, I decided on one. Family comedy. I let go of my idea of what I liked at the movies — that was for me *after* work. Instead I embraced what I could *do*. And family comedies came easily to me. I saw that as my service, my specialty, my strength. And now I began searching the trades, reading about the sales of spec screenplays in that category, trying to figure out how to make mine like theirs. It was a focus bordering on being laser-like, and yet by doing so, by cutting out everything that was not that, I saw how someone might be helped if they ever actually hired me.

How was I positive? Well, I wasn't always. There were blue days. That's life. But like every part of my new regimen, if I failed, I did not berate myself for it and call my day a failure. I knew I'd try to do better tomorrow. And it worked. One time that summer I was set to have a meeting with a producer, but it wasn't until I drove the hour and a half to Los Angeles that I learned the meeting was off. Calling to break the news to my agent, I tried to be chipper — and because of my attitude, she invited me to lunch. And it was during that lunch that much of the rest of that year was planned out. By being away from L.A., I was realizing how many opportunities I'd wasted when I lived there, and now made up my mind to make sure I took advantage of every one that came my way.

And when I did feel down, I'd take walks by myself along State Street, sometimes late at night. And as I did, I would silently repeat my mantra in time with my step — *Discipline, Focus, and Positive Energy* — while imagining what the world would look like if I did succeed. And as I walked, I realized that other part I had read about, the part in my father's books that he sought, which was now being confirmed to me: I wasn't alone. I never was.

The best part of that summer was my relationship with my agent, Hilary Wayne, but that too was part of the serendipity. When I got the job to write for Tommy Lynch, I desperately needed every cent. But I also knew what an opportunity this was to secure an agent, so I offered Hilary the commission for taking me on. She had just been hired by Joan Scott at Writers & Artists Agency as an assistant, and with my deal and a few others, she was promoted to agent. We were the same age, at the same stage of our careers, Hilary and I. And as focused as I was on cracking this thing, she was doubly so — and fearless! The day she became an agent, she went to Universal, talked her way onto the lot, and knocked on doors introducing herself to executives. She was the new rep at Writers & Artists, just stopping by to say "hi."

And so the summer went.

At night, with the pounding sound of music and partying coming from below my office, I no longer needed to be in public to write. I was *writing*. Across the street was a movie theater, with some Spanishy-name the Santa Barbara town fathers loved — which Jim Haggin waggishly dubbed "The El Pacino" — and with every movie that came out, I was right there, studying trailers, talking to other moviegoers to find out why they went and if they enjoyed it... and why. And when Hilary called with a meeting she'd set up, I'd go rent every movie that director or producer had anything to do with, and drove down to Los Angeles for each meeting — ready to talk about any project they had, ready to do anything to figure out how I could offer service, because that's what I discovered my job was all about.

That summer I learned how to be a professional writer. I made it a job I took seriously. I focused on my goals and tried hard to look at each day as half full. And I kept at it.

People would come visit me in my white-walled suite. I had only a desk, a stand for my printer, and a couch in two big rooms. I blocked the windows so I wouldn't have distractions. And I kept at it. I figured out Hollywood goes to lunch at 1:00 and got in sync with their schedule. By fall, I was an office-hours-keeping, full-time writer bearing down on success... but still not finding it.

Then one fine morning, Hilary called and said there was a bidding war on my latest script. "Don't answer the phone!" she said mysteriously. And I held my breath. All day. And paced. At 5:30 that afternoon, Hilary called to say she'd sold my script for $300,000 against $500,000 and was really proud of me and couldn't talk just now because she was off to the Rolling Stones concert that night, but I'd have the check in two days. "Bye!"

From April to October of that crossroads year, with help from Jim Haggin, I'd figured out how to write a saleable script.

Within three years, I had co-written not only one spec screenplay with Jim that sold for a million dollars, but two.

And within four years, I was living back in Los Angeles, with a two-picture deal at Disney and an office on the lot, going into production on a movie I not only co-wrote but co-executive produced with my great, good friend, Hilary Wayne.

It was during the celebration for that sale Hilary smiled at me and said: Can you believe this is really happening?

Yes! I said out loud. But in truth, I had no idea.

SAVE THE CAT! GOES TO CHINA

For those of you who don't like "Tales of the Impossible," I hear ya. There's nothing worse than some happy dufus with a headset standing on stage telling you the Six Keys to Success.

But that's why I'm just keeping it between you and me.

I don't have to prove anything, and neither do you, but I promised to tell you everything; I vowed up front I would take it to the max in my effort to give you every tool I've used and let you pick and choose the ones you try, when you want to try them.

My goals are not your goals, and should not be. Only you know what has been placed in your heart and what you yearn to achieve. I think one of the amazing things about this, however, is we can never ask for too much, or be surprised by who steps forward to help us achieve our goals. I don't know exactly how to say this, but the specifics of why it happens isn't any of our business. We do our part, and that's all we can do. And I totally understand that for many of you... this borders on the woo-woo. It's not my place to go much beyond here. Your mileage may vary. But in case you're *still* not a believer, try this on for size:

When I spoke at Screenwriting Expo in 2008, I titled my talk "Supercharge!" I was gathering notes for this chapter, too, and knew I'd be using that part of my life as an example, and as inspiration. I remembered keeping my diary, and that ridiculous — seemingly — first entry. I dug the orange notebook out and read through it in the nostalgic way we do, thinking about that day, that meeting, that thought that seemed so vital at the time. And then perusing further, I found an entry that startled me:

"As part of giving back for achieving my goals, I will write a book about how to write a screenplay," I declared. "It will have the Rules of Screenwriting as I've discovered them and be called '*The Method: The Ultimate Screenwriter's Guide* by Blake Snyder.' Here are things I will talk about [that I] learned..."

- ▶ Turn, Turn, Turn
- ▶ The Pope in the Pool — exposition
- ▶ Eyepatch and Limp — characters
- ▶ Dialogue — "Hi, how are you? I'm fine"

Again, let me emphasize, I hadn't sold a screenplay when I wrote those words. Yet within that entry is the beginning of what I would write about years later in *Save the Cat!* I also note that right below that entry, written as an afterthought, was this:

"Needs better title."
No kidding.

It had been 10 years or more since I'd picked up that notebook and glanced through it, and again, I can't express the outrageousness of making the claim. And yet, seeing it now, I also know that it was the other part of the training I had received that summer. The idea of achieving the impossible, of turning something intangible into something concrete, is real.

And forever surprising.

I have a whole new set of goals on my wall now — some that shock even me. But right next to them is my second card listing:

▸ *Discipline*
▸ *Focus*
▸ *Positive Energy*

Because one card without the other is just wishing.

And you never know where this stuff will take you.

Because of *Save the Cat!* I've taught all over the world. The ultimate trip, so far, was Beijing, China. By invitation of officials there, who'd read my book and were inspired by it, I was asked to lecture to the top filmmakers in the country. Along with my translator, Feng Wen, and with a lot of help from American producer Kevin Geiger, the trip was a great success.

I even have slides!

Just hanging out with my *Cats!*
What an amazing ride!

I walked The Great Wall with my two books. I toasted Mr. Jing, a key figure in the Ministry of Culture who decides which 20 American films are shown in China each year (as he told me, Mr. Jing can get anyone in Hollywood on the phone any time). And I taught the principles of communication that *Cat!* is known for, and showed why the simple tools it examines apply all over the globe.

That's our world now. And that's our market.

Yet the underlying principles are the same everywhere.

Because we are human, all of us — all over the globe — are drawn to stories of transformation. And part of transformation is death. That's what this book has really been about, if you haven't guessed, that moment where we are faced with a brick wall — the death of loved ones, or the death of our old ideas — and we must embrace the new to survive... and thrive. Hitting the wall in a script is good for us because it makes us more human; any death we experience, and any failure will — that's why we must embrace it, even look for it, and always be ready to go beyond.

During a break in my lectures in Beijing, a film student asked to speak to me and told me that I'd gotten it wrong.

I had said that the "Save the Cat!" moment was about the hero doing something nice that made us like him. But in Chinese, the phrase means something else. It's not that the hero saves the cat; it's that by saving the cat, the hero gives the cat a new life. And by doing so, she told me, the hero gets a new life, too.

My hesitation to reply wasn't that I didn't understand.

It was my being amazed by where life can take us.

For me, a guy very interested in transformation, I am always looking for the death of old ideas. And I hope you are, too. Because accepting the change that we all seek — both as writers telling stories and as audiences viewing them — is the point where we can begin to create a new life, a life beyond our wildest dreams. It starts with that moment, getting the direst possible news, or failing miserably and thinking we'll never succeed, or worse, getting everything we *think* we want and finding it's not what we wanted at all. For just around the corner from that, if we're lucky, is something remarkable, something miraculous.

And that's the transformation I wish for you.

glossary

FINAL TERMS OF ENGAGEMENT FROM THE LAND OF THE 310

ATTA BOY ▶ This is my buddy Mike Cheda's term for that little bit of encouragement every creative person needs... before we rip his or her effort to shreds. For example, "I love what you did here, and here, but..." Surprisingly controversial in that writers feel it's merely a dinner mint given us on the way to the gallows, but for me, I need a spoonful of sugar to help the medicine go down.

AT HOME, AT WORK, AND AT PLAY ▶ The world of the hero needs to be set up when we start every story. And even though not every story has these scenes exactly, it must in some form. Think about the Set-Up for Russell Crowe in *Gladiator*: *At work*, he's a great Roman General; *at home*, his wife is waiting; *at play*, the after-party of his troops' Teutonic victory reveals the depth of friendship for him in the ranks. These "Ats" show a hero's life.

BOUNCING BALL, THE ▶ What do I pay attention to when I hear or read someone's story? It's the introduction of, set-up for, and changes that happen to the hero as he transforms and grows. The "bouncing ball" I'm following is not plot, but the character at your tale's center, and the changes that occur to him along the way. Keep *your* eye on the bouncing ball — that's the story.

COVERAGE ▶ Talent agencies, producers, and studio executives don't always read the script, but have it read or "covered" by a reader. The problem for you is... coverage travels fast. Names of scripts and grades assigned them are logged and not always kept private. Letting just one industry official read your script may mean the entire town has access to his assessment. Not to get you too paranoid, but a virgin script has power that degrades every time you hand it off to someone to read... so do so wisely.

DOUBLE BUMP ▶ This is my magic getter-out-of-trouble when a plot with either a lot of "pipe" or a hero who must be pushed requires a couple of nudges to move into Act Two. Normally, only one "invitation" is required at Catalyst, something done *to* the hero. But if you need a second at Break into Two, bump away!

DOUBLE DIPPING ▶ This is the no-no managers and their clients should avoid. It means a manager takes both a 15% manager's fee and a producer's fee for a script that he helped to set up. It's one or the other, never both. Along with the "reading fees" that some agents request to vet a script, about as despicable, double dipping will lead to pained cries of "conflict of interest"!

DRAFT AND A SET, A ▶ Typically this is the agent's term for a standard rewrite deal. It means you will get to write one "draft" of said script, plus a "set" of polish notes. This does not necessarily guarantee anything other than a minimum of both work and payment for it — provided you show up with a smile and do your best.

ELEMENT ▶ This is the project booster that can get a movie made or a script read. It can be an actor, director, financier, or special effects house — anything tacked onto a screenplay that makes it seem easier to make or pay for. An element is not always the dream it seems, as sometime other elements object.

ELEVATOR PITCH ▶ Be advised: There is no elevator. This is the imaginary situation where you have two to three floors, about 20 seconds, to tell your movie idea to the imaginary executive who rides in these elevators. Can you fascinate him or her — fast — without resorting to pushing the Emergency Stop?

EXTERNAL AND INTERNAL ▶ These are the twin skeins of action found in the Bad Guys Close In section of a script in which both external and internal pressure is applied to make our hero change — exactly what he is resisting! Having a sense of oncoming "death" in the All Is Lost moment, heroes resist both the external and internal, but cannot do so for long.

FORCED CONFLICT ▶ Why do so many movie scenes involve two characters shouting at each other? Why do strange encumbrances occur to "force" those characters to even be there — trapped... and screaming? It's because the screenwriter needs to amp up the conflict of EVERY scene, because conflict is why we came. If it's not in every scene, the audience will... *zzzzz*...

"FORCE IT!" ▶ This is the handy phrase I use in class and in working with writers to get them to "hit their marks" as dramatists. We don't care if you the writer think it's obvious or overly simple or clichéd or any number of excuses... hit your marks! When you feel you can't, try harder. We the audience expect drama, we expect to see transformation, we expect a story!

"HERE'S THE BAD WAY TO DO THIS" ▶ The other handy phrase that goes along with "Force it!" is the one that lets reluctant writers off the hook. Are you stalled, mired in not having a solution to a story point, character arc, or way to tell the theme? Give yourself an excuse to present a solution that might sound lame with "Here's the bad way to do this." It might even be great!

IN PLAY ▶ The heady cry that goes out along Agency Row that some hot bit of talent may actually be open to new representation. Let the wining and dining begin! If you're a writer, a milder form of this frenetic buzz may also be heard. Normally agents don't poach another agent's roster, but a well-placed rumor or an out-and-out phone call from the talent's other reps (lawyer, manager, personal trainer) may mean the pursuit can begin.

MOMENT OF CLARITY, THE ▶ Every hero has a period of collapse around All Is Lost. Boom. He's done. And in Dark Night of the Soul, since we've got his attention and he has nowhere else to go anyway, this is the moment where the "penny drops" and he says: "I get it!" This beat reveals all the hero's flaws in his own eyes, and though it looks like he will never get a chance to capitalize on this… we know better, don't we boys and girls?

ON THE VERGE OF... ▶ The "Hamburger Helper" for loglines kicks off any one-line plot with a sense of where the hero is, and what he wants from life when this movie starts. It also implies that the ending will be 180 degrees opposite by the time the story's over — because changing one's goal, and ideas, is the point of any tale we tell.

OPEN ASSIGNMENTS BOOK ▶ It's a binder really, three-hole punched and constantly updated by assistants at most talent agencies and management companies to track which studios are looking for which writers for which projects that need fixing. Sometimes it's a polish, sometimes a "Page One," and sometimes dozens, yes, dozens of writers will apply for the assignment.

PACKAGE ▸ This is kind of an '80s or '90s phrase, very Mike Ovitz, very CAA, but it still applies. Usually a management firm or agency doubles or triples its fees by tacking on other elements to a project they represent. Having inside knowledge and a relationship with producers and studios helps create packages.

PITCHES, REWRITES, AND GET-TO-KNOW YA'S ▸ There are three different types of meetings a writer will be sent out on by an agent. If you have a movie *pitch*, but no script yet, the writer will be matched up with a producer who will "take it in" to a studio, hopefully for a sale. *Rewrites* are projects that may not be in the Open Assignments book, and *Get-to-Know Ya's* are casual get-togethers that can lead to business, and get serious fast, if the parties involved click.

SELLING PAST THE CLOSE ▸ When you've finished your pitch, and said everything you need and planned to say when you prepared it, shut up. Smile. Sit down. Think about stuff you have to buy at Whole Foods. Think of anything but adding to the pitch you just made. If you've done your job, you're done. The ball is in their court. If you make a peep now you are… making a mistake.

SHARD OF GLASS, THE ▸ A blind spot or flaw the hero is not aware of, that sharp-edged incident, bad behavior, tough truth, or wrong done that the hero swallowed a long time ago. By the end of your tale, your hero must look at this flaw and deal with it in order to transform… and become something glorious!

SMELL OF THE RAIN ON THE ROAD AT DAWN, THE ▸ I can be driving down the street and see a guy with a t-shirt and think *"That's* a movie!!"* Is it? Doubtful. It may be the start of an idea, the story you tell on *Letterman* about how you *got* the idea, but for now it's that thing all creative people get — if they're lucky — the beginning of art, but in and of itself, only interesting to you.

SPIDERING, HALF-STEPPING, AND BLURRY BEATS ▶ The "beating out" process can include some missteps. These terms describe three different ways to *not* tell your story. If you are suddenly telling a soap opera, that's *Spidering*. If you are moving your plot forward an inch at a time, that's *Half-Stepping*. And if you are making your plot points so slight we can't see them, especially at Midpoint and the major Breaks, that's *Blurry Beats*. All three revolve around fear. Trust your story and your skills!

SPINE OF THE STORY, THE ▶ How the hero begins, changes, and grows throughout a story — that's the spine, the thing writers and audiences track to make sure they are witness to a well-structured tale. The five questions to ask to straighten any spine are: Who's the hero? What's the problem? How does the story begin and end? What are the tangible and spiritual goals? What is the story "about," what is its theme? Answer these and win.

STEALTH PRODUCERS ▶ Often a manager will put up his "shingle" (a company brand that says you're open for business in Hollywood) and attract writers to manage their careers. Not so fast! Many times these managers want more, including being "attached" as a producer to any script or project you're working on. All well and good. And very helpful. Just make sure it's okay with you.

STORMING THE CASTLE ▶ You're in Act Three and you don't know how to finish your story. This five-point plan can help sketch out any ending. Ever since posting this on my blog, I get emails from screenwriters asking: "What's my castle?" and "Who's my princess?" They may not be actual places or people, but the objective of every hero and every Finale is the same. And identifying the objectives is key to figuring out how to sum up any story.

STORY SCOLIOSIS ▶ If you have extra scenes in your screenplay that don't seem to fit; if you have D, E, and F Stories that are really interesting, but not quite germane; if you have a hero who only changes a little tiny bit in the course of your story; or if you're still going back and forth about your theme, blending three or four together… you have a crooked story spine that needs to be put up on the rack and stretched into shape. So do it.

TANGIBLE AND THE SPIRITUAL, THE ▶ There are two stories in every story: the thing that's happening on the surface, known as "plot," and the thing happening below the surface, known as "theme." The surface world is all material, *tangible* with concrete goals, obstacles, and consequences. The goals are all specific too, such as winning a trophy, a girl, or a legal case. The below-the-surface world is the *spiritual* part; it is the lesson the hero learns from the plot — and the real story. Remember: A Story = plot = wants = tangible. And B Story = theme = needs = spiritual.

THROWING IT OVER THE WALL ▶ This is my buddy Jim Haggin's term to describe getting a script to a studio so they can buy it, the idea being so good that if you "throw it over the wall" surrounding the studio, someone in charge will come across it and buy it. Not always true — especially in the 21st century — for while "concept is king" and always will be, the number of scripts and the changes in the business dictate every script that goes up for sale now be as "ready to shoot" as possible.

TOO PLAIN, TOO COMPLICATED, AND HIDING THE BALL ▶ This is the cry of development execs — and we the public — when a concept fails to fire our imaginations. As writers we are forever pitching, from initial query letters and email queries, to in-the-room pre-sentations, to the poster and trailer used to tell the public about our brilliant notion. But if you don't excite, your pitch is *too plain*. If you confuse, instead of inspire, your concept is *too complicated*, and if you are not telling us the whole story (for fear of "giving it away"), you are *hiding the ball*. Try to avoid these common pitfalls.

TRANSFORMATION MACHINE, THE ▶ Story is the ultimate transformer, and the machine that we put our heroes through to force the change makes it easier for us because it allows us to break the story down and put it back together — even while blindfolded. Each section of the story machine, from its Opening Image to Midpoint to "Moment of Clarity" to "Final Exam" to Final Image, demands change. And we must bend our stories to make sure each of these sections is being satisfied, so our hero, and our audience, are wrung out by the end.

ABOUT
THE AUTHOR

In his 20-year career as a screenwriter and producer, BLAKE SNYDER sold dozens of scripts, including co-writing *Blank Check*, which became a hit for Disney, and *Nuclear Family* for Steven Spielberg. His book, *Save the Cat!® The Last Book on Screenwriting You'll Ever Need*, was published in May 2005, and is now in its eighteenth printing. The sequel, *Save the Cat!® Goes to the Movies: The Screenwriter's Guide to Every Story Ever Told*, and software, *Save the Cat!® The Last Story Structure Software You'll Ever Need*, are also bestsellers. Along with guiding screenwriters, novelists, and other creative thinkers, Blake's method has become the secret weapon of many development executives, managers, and producers for its precise, easy, and honest appraisal of what it takes to write and develop stories in any media. Blake was a proud member of the Writers Guild of America, west. He passed away suddenly on August 4, 2009, but he lives on in his films and his books, in the advice that will never grow old, with the spirit that will continue to thrive and inspire. His story resonates with all who loved him, and your stories will resonate thanks to his love for you. Blake's vision continues on *www.blakesnyder.com*.

When Blake passed away unexpectedly on August 4, 2009, the announcement of his death on *www.blakesnyder.com* brought a storm of heartfelt comments. Here are some excerpts.

REMEMBERING BLAKE

Blake was an unstoppable force of love and inspiration.

Blake's words were golden. He was simply the best when it came to story and teaching. His books will live on forever and inspire many great writers for decades to come.

It's unlikely a day of my writing life will go by without me thinking of Blake. His contributions to understanding the nature and power of story are immeasurable. His generous nature and lively spirit will not be forgotten. The creative spark he ignited in thousands of writers will never be extinguished.

Blake had nothing but joy to offer his readers and students. He could barely contain how excited he was to share the wonders of good storytelling. Blake will not only live on as a guru who shaped countless writers, but also as a sterling example of how finding your true purpose and doing it with all your heart is the only way to live.

Here was a man in the middle of cynical Hollywood, without a trace of cynicism. He tore a joyous hole through this jaded business and he will live on.

I'm days away from finishing the first draft of the first script I've ever written with *Save the Cat!* I've been writing screenplays for 19 years (majored in screenwriting in college), and yet I've never had more fun writing a script. It is very clear from his blogs and books that he "got" not only writing, but also the writer. I believe it's this difference that makes his writing so inspiring, fun, and accessible. I know it will continue to be my guide in the future. He will not be forgotten.

Blake's books have become the template for a generation of screen-writers. His grace and style will be something that every teacher — and aren't we all teachers, at some point? — should strive to emulate.

Blake reminded me of my hopes for our films, for their capacity to change lives as well as entertain. And somehow, by breaking it down one beat at a time, he made that all seem possible.

Blake was so much more than a groundbreaking pioneer. He was the guy who held the hand of each and every one of us, telling us "Don't be afraid. I will be with you every step of the way. I'll always be here for you."

Blake made you feel like you were a welcome friend. His books and software are my favorites and the ones I've learned the most from. Blake, I am a better writer because of you. Thank you for your life, your legacy, and your love of writing.

Blake, you made such a difference in your life, something that your passing won't stop. To think how many more people you will reach through your teaching… to think the great works that will flow from the course you've set… to think the lives you will enrich through your words.

He is the #1 reason I am able to get the meetings I get and write the movies I write. There is nobody I can think of that epitomized the heart and beauty of storytelling more than Blake. His gift as both a writer and teacher is unparalleled. I will be eternally grateful for having known him and will continue to build on the skills he's given me and share them with every writer I meet until the end of my time.

Blake taught so that we could see how "brilliant" we were — not how brilliant he was.

Blake gave me such confidence in my story but he gave me more than that, he gave me a belief in myself.

Blake showed me that the power of storytelling resides within me, and his technique was the tool to bring it out. I believe this is the greatest gift he showed us all.

Let us honor this wonderful man by being the writers that he believed we were — and believing in each other.

SAVE THE CAT!® STORY STRUCTURE SOFTWARE 3.0

With the iPhone/iPod Touch and iPad versions of the bestselling *Save the Cat!®* *Story Structure Software*, you can carry your screenplay ideas with you wherever you go, so you'll be ready whenever inspiration strikes.

Structure your screenplay the *Save the Cat!®* way and create stories that resonate! This software will help you:

Develop a powerful Logline and Title.

Choose one of 10 Genres, each with recognizable traits that will help you write something that is "the same, only different."

Fill in a Blake Snyder Beat Sheet with the 15 key beats for every screenplay.

Use The Board, the fabled device seen in executive offices all over Hollywood, which allows you to "see" your movie when you **create moveable, numbered, color-coded scene cards** before you begin writing.

With a **page count** of up to 1,000, whether you're writing a short film or a long novel, the beats will appear in proportion. And with the **Save the Cat!®** Cloud, you can choose to use our Cloud to place your file into your own personal queue from which you can download it to any device or computer.